KENT
THROUGH THE YEARS

Frontispiece *High Street, Canterbury by T. S. Cooper*

KENT
through the Years

CHRISTOPHER WRIGHT

B. T. Batsford Ltd
LONDON AND SYDNEY

First published 1975
© Christopher Wright 1975
ISBN 0 7134 2881 3
Filmset by Servis Filmsetting Ltd, Manchester
Printed in Great Britain by
The Anchor Press Ltd, Tiptree, Essex
for the publishers
B. T. BATSFORD LTD.,
4 Fitzhardinge Street, London W1H 0AH
and
23 Cross Street, Brookvale, NSW, 2100 Australia

DEDICATION

To the memory of my Father, who
introduced me to Kent.

Contents

Preface

This attempt to show how the people of Kent have lived from the earliest times until today and how, in their history, they have reflected national developments makes no claim to original research or scholarship. It is based on the writings of many men and women, and those to whose works I am chiefly indebted are recorded in the reading list at the end of my book. I would, however, particularly like to acknowledge my debt to the writings of Mr Frank Jessup and to the talks given by local historians and broadcast by BBC Radio Medway during 1972–3 on the history of Kent together with the programme notes that accompanied them. Richard Harnden and Gerald Colson have helped me, particularly over the preparation of the early chapters, while my wife's criticism and encouragement have stimulated me throughout the writing of this book.

C W

Kent College
Canterbury

Acknowledgments

Jacket illustration Maidstone Museum
Kent County Education Committee: 1, 7, 11, 22, 25 (from
    F. W. Jessup's *Kent History Illustrated*)
Royal Museum, Canterbury: 2, 5, 6
Publishers collection: 3, 4, 17, 26, 28, 37, 38, 40, 41, 51, 58
    64, 65, 67
Maidstone Museum: 9, 18, 19
Ministry of the Environment: 14
London Illustrated News: 15 (by Alan Sorrell)
Bodleian Library: 16, 24
Institute of Archaeology, Oxford: 20
British Museum: 21, 23, 33–36, 44–50, 53–57, 59, 61, 62
Trinity College, Cambridge: 27
J. Allen Cash: 39
Melling & Oakley *Some Kentish Houses* (1965): 42, 43
Victoria and Albert Museum: 52
Kent County Library: 60
Tunbridge Wells Public Library: 63
Keystone Press Agency: 66

KENT

NORTH SEA

erness
Minster
hborough
Eastchurch   Warden
Leysdown
LE OF SHEPPEY
NGBOURNE   Seasalter
Whitstable
Luddenham   Graveney
nham   Oare
eet   Faversham   Dargate
Ospringe   Hernhill
Sheldwich   Boughton
Street
astling   Selling
Throwley Forstal
Thanington
Otterden   Badlesmere   Old Wives
Stalisfield   Chilham   Lees
Green
Godmersham
Charing   Petham
g Heath   Eastwell   Solestreet
Court   Crundale
Boughton Lees   Waltham
Westwell   Wye
Chart   Kennington   Elmsted   Stelling
Minnis
ASHFORD   Brook   Hastingleigh
Chart   Hinxhill   Rhodes
Brabourne   Minnis
hersden   Mersham   Smeeth   Stowting
Sellindge   Postling
Bonnington   Westenhanger
dchurch   Aldington   Lympne
Bilsington
dington
Warehorne   Newchurch   Burmarsh
oledore   Snave
Snargate   ROMNEY   Dymchurch
ne   Brenzett   MARSH
Ivychurch
rookland   Old   New Romney
Romney
WALLAND
MARSH
Lydd

HERNE BAY
Hillborough   Reculver
Herne   Sarre
Hoath   Chislet   Monkton
Upstreet
W. Stourmouth   E. Stourmouth
Blean   Sturry   Westbere   Preston
Fordwich   Elmstone
CANTERBURY   Wickhambreux
Littlebourne   Wingham   Ash
Chartham   Bekesbourne   Staple
Patrixbourne   Adisham   Eastry
Lower Hardres   Chillenden   Betteshanger
Upper   Bishopsbourne
Hardres   Barham   Tilmanstone
Barfreston   Eythorne
Denton   W. Langdon
Wootton   Lydden
Elham   Swingfield   Guston
Acrise   Ewell Minnis
Lyminge   Alkham   Houghton
Capel le   DOVER
Paddlesworth   Ferne
E. Stour
Saltwood   FOLKESTONE
Hythe   Sandgate
Royal Military Canal
Burmarsh

MARGATE
Dent-de-Lion   Broadstairs
Acol   ISLE
OF
THANET   RAMSGATE
Minster   Pegwell
Stour   Ebbsfleet Ho.
Richborough Castle
Sandwich
Woodnesborough
Worth
Deal
Mongeham   Walmer
Sutton   Kingsdown
Ringwould
St Margaret's at Cliffe
St Margaret's
Bay

STRAIT OF DOVER

Dungeness

0   5   10   15
                                 miles

Chaucer's pilgrims make their way into Canterbury

I
The Earliest Times

Any foray into the life of early man produces feelings both of wonder and frustration. We know so little, and yet what is known tells such an extraordinary story. After the interminable empty years when the earth span round without any human life at all, and rocks which are more than 1,500 million years old were formed, the emergence of an animal which experts are prepared to call man, around one million BC, seems an event of comparatively recent occurrence. And then when at last the trick is turned and the poor vulnerable upright being is here to stay, we are left marvelling, not at the unimaginable antiquity of the event so much as the unfortunate fellow's sheer survival.

Around 250,000 BC the man who has been called the first Englishman, and whose incomplete skull was found at Swanscombe, near Gravesend, appears to have lived his precarious existence. Human life in Kent had begun.

But how little, in fact we know of these early men! Our very method of classification openly confesses our ignorance. We divide them and sub-divide them again in terms of the tools they used simply because these provide the only evidence of their life we possess. It is a poor understanding of twentieth-century man which would emerge from later studies of a collection of hunting guns, electric saws, and butchers' tools. Yet some evidence is better than none, and only by their few remains can we catch glimpses of man's life in Kent at a time when probably there were no more than 250 human beings in the whole of Britain.

For the great majority of the Old Stone Age Britain was joined to the Continent of Europe by a strip of marshy land about 50 miles wide which covered the area which we now call the Straits

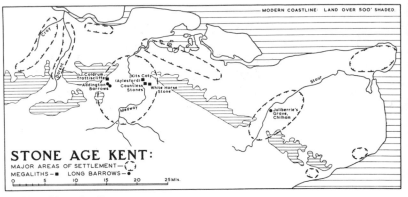

STONE AGE KENT:

MAJOR AREAS OF SETTLEMENT—◯
MEGALITHS—■   LONG BARROWS—●

0   5   10   15   20   25 Mls.

1   Map of Stone Age Kent

of Dover. The North and South Downs extended into France, and the Wealden Ridge ended in mid-Channel. Yet when around 6,000 BC, the sea broke through and separated Kent from the Pas de Calais a period was to come about, which has lasted up to the present day, in which the county's life was to be changed continually by groups of European invaders or immigrants. The sea was to prove a highway where the marsh had proved an obstacle and the pace of change was to accelerate out of all recognition.

The earliest tools which have been found in Kent are handaxes, multi-purpose instruments which were probably used as scrapers, knives, and missiles as well as axes. Similar tools were used until quite recently by Australian aborigines and are found in prehistoric sites all over the world. Handaxes have been found at Swanscombe, in the same gravel bed as the human remains, at Reculver and at Orpington, while at Cuxton, near Rochester, recent excavations have uncovered a large collection of early flint implements. Here in addition to completed handaxes, waste flakes and uncompleted axes have been found as if a workshop must have existed nearby. Flint workshops have also been found at Crayford near Dartford, in a chalk pit known as Baker's Hole at Northfleet, at Frindsbury, near Chatham, and at Bapchild, near Sittingbourne. Such workshops point to an early division of labour, and were generally situated in places where outcrops of chalk made flints readily accessible, and where water was easy to come by. As the years went by handaxes gave way to new and

12

2 Stone Age flint implements

more specialised tools—sharp points, scrapers, chopper cores, and thick flakes. Stone implements such as these have been found in various parts of the county, but particularly near river beds, such as the Thames and the Medway, along the seashore between Reculver and Whitstable, and on Oldbury Hill, at Ightham. Here the sandy soil was well drained, and the rock shelters, which must have housed an early family, provided a good view of the surrounding country. Forty-nine well-finished stone implements, and upwards of 600 waste chips of flint and numbers of flakes have been found. They were probably manufactured there. At Halling, by the Medway, a human skeleton has been found, buried in a crouching position, like a baby in the womb, head on chest, as if contemporaries regarded death as rebirth.

It is with material like this that we must compose a picture of early life in Kent. There is no reason to think that the human occupation of the county was continuous, for the climate changed with the advances and withdrawals of the ice caps whose most southerly point was in Essex. During the warm periods between the ice ages many animals lived in Kent, which are strangers to the county now. At Swanscombe remains have been found of cave bears, cave lions, wild horses, rhinoceroses, red and fallow deer,

3   *Megalith at Kit's Coty (from an eighteenth-century engraving)*

bison and straight-tusked elephants, along with traces of hippopo-
tami, brown bears, and wild oxen. During the ice ages mammoths
(part of a tusk was found at Tankerton), woolly rhinoceroses
(part of a jaw was found in the same area), reindeer, musk-ox,
lemming, arctic fox and Irish Elk were to be seen. Probably the
human settlements vanished during the long centuries of cold and
wet, but in the end they returned. Living as parasites in small
groups, hunting, fishing, and fowling, eating nuts and berries,
wild fruit and shell fish, eggs and insects, wandering over the
county and camping mainly by rivers or sheltering in caves and
rock shelters, the first men survived their appalling environment
thanks mainly to the size of their brains and their development of
speech. At last, when forests replaced the sub-arctic flora, and
the land bridge crumbled before the twin forces of rising sea-level
and sinking land which accompanied the final retreat of the ice-
cap, new inventiveness rejuvenated them. Forest creatures were
hunted with new methods. Bows and arrows were tipped with
small flints, while axes and adzes were further developed for
felling trees and constructing dug-out canoes.

Around 4,000 years ago men from Europe began to come into
Britain who brought with them a life of a radically new type. No
longer was man a mere animal of prey. He became a farmer, a

creative settler. Though they had no knowledge of metals these men used stone tools of considerable sophistication which enabled them not only to improve greatly upon their predecessors' hunting and fishing activities but also to grow and reap crops—the earliest of which were wheat and barley—and to clear forest land on the more easily worked soils. They domesticated animals, particularly cattle and pigs, built single-roomed houses, engaged in a trade in flints which covered England and Wales and extended even to northern Ireland and left behind them elaborately constructed graves. Kent has ample evidence of these peoples' lives and it is clear that the county began now to be much more heavily populated than ever before.

Judging from their burial stones, or megaliths, these men would seem to have come from Denmark, northern Germany, and north-east Holland and to have either settled along the county's coasts or to have moved inland by way of the main rivers. Evidence of their settlement is particularly strong in the area of the Medway Valley around Aylesford, where the ford through the river led to sandy soil and chalky scrubland.

The surviving megaliths were built as parts of the long graves known as barrows, mounds of earth or rubble since destroyed, leaving behind them only these stone constructions which once served as vaults beneath them or perhaps, as at Kits Coty, a false doorway to mislead grave robbers. They are made of local boulders called sarsen, and are to be found near Aylesford, to the

4   *Coldrum Long Barrow, near Trottiscliffe (*c. 2000 BC*)*

east of the Medway around Kits Coty, and to the west near Trottiscliffe at Coldrum and at Addington. At Coldrum the remains of 22 people of both sexes and of varying ages have been found, probably members of the same family group. The bones would seem to indicate a long-headed rather short people, with teeth that met edge-to-edge, and muscles of only moderate strength, whose old people suffered from rheumatism.

The main evidence for the construction of Neolithic huts or, to be more precise, hut floors, comes from Hayes Common, about five miles from Bromley. Here large pits have been found which are up to 30 feet in diameter and up to two feet six inches deep. They are surrounded with a mound which contains an entrance, and sometimes have in their middle a low conical construction, which may well have been the foundation for a roof support to cover the hut. The dwellings were built in groups of from four to six, and each could take from between two and six people. Separate smaller pits, containing reddened pebbles and fragments of charred wood must have been used as cooking holes, and it seems that the fire was made on a large scale and maintained for a long time so as to make the earth sufficiently hot to cook whole animals. Cattle pens were placed outside the settlements and guarded, like the hut floors, with a wooden stockade.

Evidence that the peoples in Kent at this time were in touch with groups all over Britain is to be found in the origin of stone axes discovered in the county. An axe found at New Hythe originates from Penmaenmawr (Caernarvonshire), an adze at Dartford Heath from the Lake District, an axe-hammer found at Ramsgate comes from Cornwall, and an axe discovered at Sittingbourne has travelled from County Antrim in northern Ireland. At Canterbury the discovery of a jadeite axe similar to those manufactured in Brittany and a flint axe from Scandinavia would seem to indicate trade or perhaps war with Europe. As for the development of stone tools a visit to the Maidstone Museum quickly reveals the skill of the Neolithic craftsmen—flint sickles for reaping and saddle querns for grinding corn, very fine leaf-shaped arrowheads, polished chisels, and flint axes with polished cutting edges are evidence of impressive specialisation. In addition, rough pottery of the same period can be seen, such as a pottery spoon from Ightham, along with holed stones probably used as hammer heads or net sinkers for fishing, or weights for the digging sticks

5   *Beakers of about 1900–1500 BC*

which formed the primitive ploughs. It is clear that the areas where Neolithic settlement was most intense—such as Thanet, the Dour Valley behind Dover, a strip of land under the Downs near Folkestone, along the Stour, Darent and Cray valleys, the North-Kent chalkland east of Horton Kirby (a village between Dartford and Fawkham) and above all the lower Medway Valley—all witnessed ways of life which are the first in the county to warrant the adjective 'civilised'.

Although Kent had now become more populated, great stretches of the county remained largely unsettled and this was to continue to be the case long after the peoples from the Rhineland whom we call the 'Beaker' people from their pottery began entering the area around 1700 BC. Despite their improved implements they too were to avoid the North Downs, which were heavily wooded and had little water. As for the Weald, the heavy wet clay soil nourished a thick and terrifying forest, running south of a line from Tonbridge to Ashford, which was to cut Kent off from the rest of England lying to the south-west, until the middle ages. The new peoples brought with them bronze tools, but do not at first seem to have known how to make them themselves. Stone implements remained easily the most common and they continued to improve, as contemporary axes, flint knives, and delicate barbed arrow-heads show. After several hundred years the new tribes began to manufacture bronze axes of various types, spear-

6 Bronze Age tools and weapons

heads, sickles, hammers, knives, gouges, and finally swords, many
of which show the highest skill in craftsmanship. Leaf-shaped
swords, two feet long, rapiers and dirks of about the same length
and daggers found in a grave at Aylesford testify to their technical
skill, as do the pots which have given these people their name.
These were used domestically and for use as burial urns, and were
elaborately patterned. They have been found in graves along the
coast or in the Medway and Stour valleys at Maidstone, Chislet,
Sturry and Canterbury.

The use of bronze testifies to the amount of trade which must
have been conducted, and reminds one of the earlier trade in
stone axes. The copper used came from Ireland, or from northern
or western Britain, the tin from Europe or from Cornwall. Twelve
or so hoards of bronze implements have been found in Kent and
those discovered at Marden and Swalecliffe can be seen in Maidstone Museum. Some were buried with the graves of chiefs, but
more must have belonged to bronzesmiths, for lumps of unworked
metal have been found with the tools. The largest hoard has been
found at Minster-in-Thanet and can be seen in the British
Museum. It contained 143 objects made of bronze, among them
axes, swords, spearheads, and sickles. Probably the bronzesmith
was itinerant, and did the circuit of his area, repairing old tools,
making and selling new. Even more remarkable than the bronze
work that has been found are the gold ornaments which have been
discovered in various parts of Kent. The gold probably came from

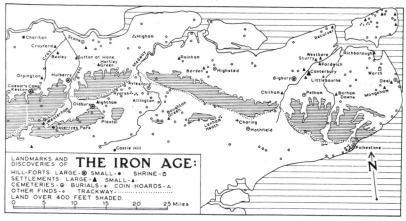

LANDMARKS AND DISCOVERIES OF **THE IRON AGE:**
HILL-FORTS: LARGE-◎ SMALL-● SHRINE-□
SETTLEMENTS: LARGE-▲ SMALL-▲
CEMETERIES-◉ BURIALS-+ COIN·HOARDS-⚹
OTHER·FINDS-○ TRACKWAY-⋯⋯⋯⋯⋯
LAND OVER 400 FEET SHADED.
0   5   10   15   20   25 Miles

N

7   *Iron Age Kent*

Ireland, and the ornaments can be seen at their most impressive in the display case in the Maidstone Museum, where superbly wrought late Bronze Age neck-rings and bracelets, one with a remarkable trumpet shape, found in a chief's grave near Aylesford, are on show.

The Beaker people too settled most extensively in the Medway and Stour valleys, and along the coast. They utilized convenient river crossings such as at Aylesford and Canterbury, using Chatham as a suitable landing place for entry to the Medway area. They further extended the already considerable area of their ancestors' trade, cleared more land, went on living as farmers and as hunters, improving their techniques at both, developed boat-building, pottery and craftsmanship in metals, and devoted considerable attention to the perfection of weapons which must have been used in warfare with their fellow human beings as well as for killing animals.

The iron-using tribes who entered Kent from Europe between 500 and 450 BC lived much the same lives as their predecessors, though the pace of technical change was regularly increasing. They were farmers, and seem to have been peaceful men, who moved up the rivers and along the ridgeways, avoiding heavy undrained soil, and establishing their wattle-and-daub farmsteads on light land. During the third century BC they were attacked by invaders from northern France, and constructed a series of hill forts, all of which are in the western part of the county except for

19

Bigbury, near Canterbury. The largest fort covers an area of 123
acres and is on the crest of a hill at Oldbury, near Ightham. The
invaders' settlements at Margate, Dumpton Gap, Worth and
Walmer have been investigated. Pottery of a type found by the
Marne in North France has been discovered, and the new colonists seem to have imposed their rule on the earlier inhabitants by
force. Finally, around 100 BC, a new series of invaders settled in
Kent, the Belgae. These are the people who offered such effective
resistance to Julius Caesar's raids in strength, in 55–54 BC, and
whose life can be far more effectively reconstructed than that of
any previous invader.

The Belgaes' ancestors had come originally into northern
France from across the Rhine about 200 BC and this may explain
Caesar's suggestion that their language was linked with that of
Germanic tribes. Nevertheless, the general view seems to be that
the languages spoken in Kent from the fourth century BC or before
were forms of Celtic, ancestral to Welsh, and indeed some Celtic
names have survived such as the rivers Darent, meaning the
'oak-river', and Dour (Dover) meaning stream. (*Dwfr* in modern
Welsh means water.) All traces of pre-Celtic languages have
disappeared. The iron-age men used a trackway which has become
famous under the name of the Pilgrims' Way, but which in fact
was used many hundreds of years before pilgrims moved along it
on the way to Becket's tomb at Canterbury. It is more accurate to

9 *Bronze Age handle mount in the form of a mask found at Boughton Aluph, First Century BC*

call it by its modern long-distance footpath name—for it has recently been opened up by the Countryside Commission—and to call it the North Downs Way. It started north of Folkestone and followed the southern ridge of the North Downs across the Stour, along past Boughton Aluph and Charing, to cross the Medway near Aylesford, there to follow the line of the hills, passing north of Oldbury and Ightham to ford the Darent and to leave the county via Westerham. It moved through Surrey and Hampshire until it reached the sea at Southampton and along it contact of all sorts, particularly commercial, was established between Kent and the rest of southern England.

The Belgae seem to have established control over much of Kent fairly quickly. Their main headquarters in East Kent was at Canterbury and they used the nearby hill fort at Bigbury as a settlement. It has been carefully excavated, and the finds reveal a manner of life which is the most technically efficient yet to be known in the county. The camp stood on the line of the North Downs Way and overlooked the Stour Valley. There was a large and separate cattle compound to the north of it. The settlers used a heavy iron plough, which could turn much heavier soil than any earlier implements and with which they prepared the ground for wheat, barley, and possibly oats. These crops were reaped with sickles, and the harvest was brought home in carts with iron-tyred wheels. They knew a certain amount about carpentry, to judge from the chisels, gouges, and adzes that have been found, and with their bill hooks they cleared the forests more extensively than ever before. The bridlebits, harness equipment, and horse-shoes which have been found show that the Belgae were the first men to use horses in Kent, both domestically and for war. Plenty of pottery, now being turned on the wheel, has survived, and the iron tripods, pothooks, and fire dogs testify to their methods of cooking.

Excavations of iron-age farmsteads at Sturry and Fordwich near Canterbury have shown that the farmers lived in timber-framed wattle-and-daub huts within an enclosure. Household refuse left behind by contemporary Belgic settlers in Canterbury reveal their diet. There are bones of cows, sheep, and pigs. Antlers from deer and remains of wild boars come probably from the surrounding forests, while the mussel and oyster shells originate from the Thames and Stour estuaries. Before and after Caesar's attacks the Belgae traded regularly with their fellow countrymen across the Channel. According to the Roman geographer, Strabo, who lived from 64 BC to 21 AD, they exported slaves to Europe, and discoveries at Bigbury would support his evidence. An iron chain of neck-collars linked together, 18 feet long, two fetters, and a barrel lock for the slave's collar could have been used for nothing else. But the best evidence for trade with Europe well before the Roman raids is contained in the coins which have been found in fairly large numbers, particularly along the line of the North Downs Way, and on the coast between Minster and Deal. The earliest finds are from the late second century BC, and are modelled on the fourth century coin the stater of Philip II of Macedon with the wreathed head of Apollo on one side, and a two-horse chariot on the other. The coins were at first minted in north France, but later they were made in Britain, and towards the end of the first century BC they contained the names of kings. Coins struck during the reign of King Cuno-belinus for instance, who ruled south-east Britain from 5 BC to 43 AD, show an ear of corn with the inscription CAMV, standing for Camulodunum (Colchester), the king's capital and mint.

The picture of Belgic life which we have reconstructed from the work of the archeologists is confirmed by the accounts which Julius Caesar left behind of his two attacks on Kent in 55 and 54 BC. His main motive for mounting an expedition across the Channel, he tells us, was punitive: '. . . Caesar' (he always wrote about himself in the third person) 'made active preparations for an expedition to Britain, because he knew that in almost all the Gallic campaigns the Gauls had received reinforcements from the Britons.'

If Belgic resistance had been less determined, if the Gallic tribes which the Romans had conquered had been less likely to revolt the moment the bulk of their conqueror's forces had safely sailed across the Channel, if his own ambitions had not lain in Rome itself, and if, above all, he had discovered the fine natural harbour of Richborough, he might well have decided to make the usual thorough Roman bid for colonisation. But he delayed his first start until late in August 55 BC, had great difficulty in getting ashore at Deal, for the Belgae were well prepared to receive him, left his fleet on those open shelving beaches, and saw many of his transports smashed by storm. He was, indeed, fortunate to extricate himself from a situation which might well have ended in disaster, and returned to northern France fairly quickly, though his troops had defeated the Belgae in open engagement. He returned again the next year and landed at the same place with more than the original 10,000 infantry, supported by 4,000 Gallic cavalry. This time his men marched quickly inland and stormed Bigbury. But again his fleet was badly damaged by storm, and he was forced to return to Deal for 10 days to organise repairs. During his absence the Belgic tribes in Kent put all their forces under the command of their compatriot King Cassivellaunus, chief of the Catuvellauni tribe which had previously crossed the Thames and established its head-quarters at Wheathampstead, near St Albans. Caesar marched inland, crossed the Thames—probably at Brentford— attacked and captured Wheathampstead, and forced Cassivellaunus' surrender in August. But again Caesar was keen to return across the Channel before the autumn gales, and he did so with all his men. He never returned and the Romans were to leave Britain alone for nearly a hundred years.

Caesar described the tribes of Kent as living a life which in most particulars resembled that of their cousins in northern Gaul. The county's population was said to be large, and the ground thick with homesteads, where many cattle were penned. Bronze or gold coins, or iron ingots, circulated as currency, and there was tin inland. There were ample crops of corn, and the skill and ferocity of the Belgic charioteers severely shook the Roman legions' nerve. The Belgae were clearly highly skilled handlers of horses.

For the next 90 years contact between the Roman Empire and Kent increased. Indeed, some Romans argued that there was no need to conquer Britain, as they gained through trade with the country all conceivable advantages. Mass-produced red glazed pottery made in Gaul has been found in considerable quantities in the county. It was made between Caesar's raids and the Claudian occupation. Large wine vessels from Italy, southern France, and Spain have also been discovered. During this time the tribes took to fighting among themselves, and Kent became part of Cunobelinus' territory which stretched north-west from the Essex coast to Cambridge, and south again to the Weald. The signs are that his court became increasingly Romanised, and there were numbers of Roman traders living in Britain. Two of Cunobelinus' sons, however, were adopting an anti-Roman line and there were fears that they might attack north Gaul, when their father died. The Romans, who were now more secure internally and who had troops to spare, planned an expedition from Boulogne in AD 40 which was abandoned. When Cunobelinus died, one of his sons fled into exile in the Roman Empire, to appeal for help. The Emperor Claudius sent Aulus Plautius with 40,000 men to conquer Britain. He landed at Richborough unopposed. This time the invaders were here to stay.

2

Roman Kent

The choice of the little island of Richborough, in the Wantsum
Channel, as a base assured the formidable invasion forces of
success. At this time, and for many hundreds of years to come,
Thanet was separated from the rest of Kent by a broad and navigable strip of sea in which Richborough stood, close to the main-
land. The Channel provided that large and sheltered anchorage
for Roman ships which Caesar had so urgently required, while the
island was large enough to be used not just as a landing ground
but as an invasion base. The British had not opposed the landing.
The Romans threw up earthern banks around the base and moved
inland.

The Kentish tribes were not united and, even under Cunobelinus, the chiefs had been largely independent. Cunobelinus' sons
Caractacus—often called Caradog, a common Welsh name still
today—and Togodumnus, hurried to East Kent but the Belgic
forces were defeated twice before the Romans reached the
Medway. Here the decisive battle occurred, probably around
Rochester, where the Britons had destroyed the bridge over the
Medway. Some Roman troops, including the cavalry, swam
across the river at this point, but the bulk marched along the bank
of the river until they found a spot where they could ford it,
probably around Burham and Snodland. Then they turned back
to attack the Belgic forces who were drawn up in the hills to the
west of the Rochester crossing. They combined with the cavalry,
who attacked frontally, and a two day battle followed. In the end
the Belgae were broken and fled towards the Thames. A fortnight
later the Romans had crossed that river and occupied the Belgic
stronghold of Colchester. Kent had been conquered beyond any

10   Roman coins from Dover Castle

further questioning. There were no resistance movements operating against the conquerors in the years ahead.

The Roman method of colonisation was one in which an obvious military presence was avoided wherever possible. The legions were stationed along the border with Scotland, or in areas of determined resistance like Wales. In Kent they established a large military depot at Richborough, built a fort at the other end of the Wantsum at Reculver, and perhaps garrisoned some troops at Springhead, near Gravesend. Little else was seen of the army.

Settlement of the countryside seems to have followed quickly after the Conquest, and by 100 AD the face of Kent had been transformed. The army offered a secure market for farm produce, particularly corn and meat, and there was an increase in corn exports to Europe, now that the county formed part of the Roman Empire. The remains of simple wooden huts, built shortly after the conquest, have been found within ditched boundaries. They belonged to farmers, the great majority of whom must have been British, who kept cattle, sheep, and pigs and grew corn on farms which averaged around 50 acres. Within a generation after the Conquest the first 'villas'—more like medieval manor houses, centres of large estates, than modern country houses—had

26

developed. At Eccles, near Maidstone, a simple Roman strip-house villa, containing 10 or more rooms, opening out of each other, and a verandah, had been built by 65 AD. At Faversham, around 100 AD, the descendants of a Belgic farmer built themselves their first villa, which was excavated fairly recently. It contained four rooms divided by a passage, which ran from front to back. Later wide corridors were built on at the side of the original building, with large rooms, gaily decorated. Later again a new south wing was added, with a mosaic floor of coloured stones, and underfloor heating. Some villa owners would have been Roman civil servants, commuting to Canterbury or London, but more seem to have been prominent Britons who had been delighted to adopt a Roman style of life.

Romano-British Kent throughout its long history contained a variety of settlements, living alongside each other. Ordinary British life often continued in much the same way. The same language—the forerunner of modern Welsh and Breton—was spoken, though any Briton who could write did so in Latin. The life of Celtic villages and farms remained basically unaltered. It was the British aristocrat or wealthy farmer and the Briton who found himself being drawn into the Roman towns whose way of life was most deeply affected. But most Britons remained apart and reverted to type when the Romans left.

For all that, agricultural changes occurred which can genuinely

11   *Roman–British Kent*

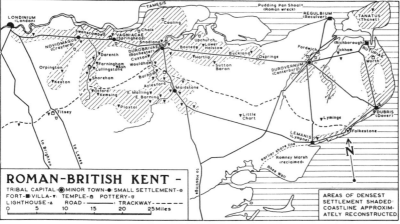

27

12 Artist's impression of Lullingstone, c. 360

be called revolutionary. The landlords and the farmers may have been mainly British, but they adopted Roman ways. On the large villas, the land immediately around the house was cultivated by slaves, while much of the rest of the estate was let to *coloni*, who were in roughly the same position as medieval serfs. Other estates were farmed by bailiffs, whose houses are to be found close to the Great House. Some of the farms were farmed by freeholders and some by tenant farmers. Some villas may well have been farmed in conjunction with other land owned by the same landowner, and others were lived in by officials, who relaxed in the country, when they were not occupying their town houses. Some of the labour was slave, some serf, some free. All contributed to the transformation of agriculture, away from the self-sufficient farming of pre-Conquest Kent to a system of surplus farming, whose markets in the towns and in the army provided a steady incentive to improved methods.

Settlement was heaviest in the areas where one would expect it to be so—along the coast opposite France, along Watling Street and the south bank of the Thames, and in the Darent, Cray and

13   The 'Europa' panel from the Lullingstone mosaic

Medway valleys. The Weald, although iron was being mined there from the beginning of the period, was left largely alone—an area 120 miles long and 20 miles broad—and the valley of the Stour only intensively settled within a five mile radius of Canterbury. About 60 villas have been found in all, some of which clearly stood at the centre of an estate which covered many hundreds of acres. Two are particularly impressive, Lullingstone and Darenth.

Lullingstone stood on a terrace cut into the hillside overlooking the Darent river, eight miles or so north of modern Sevenoaks,

14 *'The Lullingstone Christian' wall painting (Fourth Century AD)*

with its garden running down to the river. At the height of its prosperity it must have looked like a very large, leisurely spaced modern bungalow, with a roof made of heavy red tiles, flanking wings built onto it, and a cluster of farm buildings around the home. The walls were built of flint and mortar on a framework of wooden beams and were painted inside with highly coloured designs. In the centre of the complex stood dining and reception rooms, with mosaic floors, lit by glazed windows placed high up in the wall. There was, as usual, a private bath house, and among the outbuildings was a large granary built close to the river with a thatched roof, farm buildings, and two pagan temples. The farm covered many hundreds of acres. Corn was grown on the rising downland behind the house, the woods provided oak for the estate carpenter, fuel for the bath house fires, and acorns for the herds of swine, while the cattle and horses could graze along the river banks. The river could be used for transporting produce directly to the Thames, and the road which ran up the valley from the estate joined Watling Street five miles away. Though Lullingstone's fortunes varied dramatically, at its height the villa must have stood at the centre of a most prosperous and efficient farm system. The surrounding Darent valley is thought to have contained more Roman settlements than any comparable valley in England, including the Cotswolds. The villa's owners seem to have felt no need to fortify their property against attack. The well, for instance, stands unprotected outside the cluster of buildings. Such prosperity and such confidence had never been seen before in Kent, nor were they to be seen again until Tudor times. But Lullingstone's main claim to Kentish, and indeed to national fame, lies in the discovery that it housed a Christian chapel built about 365 above a room where pagan worship still continued. On the plaster of the chapel walls are figures painted in the attitude of men at prayer and a large painting of the Christian sign—the Chi Rho monogram. When the villa was abandoned as a country house, it was still used for Christian worship until finally, in the fifth century, the buildings were destroyed by fire.

At nearby Darenth another large manor house stood close to the river, with outbuildings, a bath-building, and a bailiff's house built around it. Here a block of buildings, originally probably a corridor house, with a set of baths and a hypocaust room built close to it was turned into a large-scale factory for fulling, and

15 Artist's impression of Roman Canterbury. 1 city walls; 2 North gate; 3 Quenin Gate; 4 Road to Richborough; 5 Temple; 6 Forum; 7 Theatre; 8 Town House, Butchery Lane; 9 Bath Buildings; 10, 13, 14 Town Houses; 11, 15–18 Streets; 12 Baths

probably also the dyeing of cloth. The gardens, like the estates, were on the grand scale; some seem to have been walled, others ornamental. There was a separate guest house, and a swimming pool. Like the villa at Keston, near Bromley, it seems likely that the Darenth Great House was lived in at times by a leading Roman civil servant working in London, 15 miles away.

The Roman authorities were accustomed to town life and set about, early in their period of occupation, the construction of new and impressive towns at Colchester and St Albans, which had been tribal centres before the invasion. Kent, perhaps because the county was quickly and decisively defeated, had no town which could be compared with these or other Roman towns, like London, Lincoln, York, or Gloucester. But Canterbury, the tribal capital, grew quickly after the invasion. The town acted as a focus for local life. It stood at a point where several vital roads met and crossed the river Stour—the Watling Street from Richborough which ran through Canterbury to London and the north-west, and the roads from the coastal forts of Lympne, Dover, and Reculver which joined Watling Street at Canterbury. It also stood close to the furthest navigable point of the Stour, like London in relation to the Thames, for the river below Canterbury in those days widened like a V-shaped estuary to reach the Wantsum Channel and the open sea 10 miles away.

At its height Roman Canterbury covered about 130 acres. Its straight streets were carefully planned, in the usual logical Roman way, with one street running at right angles into another. There was no feeling of crush within the walls. The well-to-do lived in comfortable town houses, spaced round their own court-yards, which would often contain a garden. Such a town house stood in present day Butchery Lane, where its mosaic floor has been uncovered, and is on view to the public in the building known as the Roman Pavement. It seems to have been an extensive range of buildings, built on a simple corridor plan round a quad-rangle, late in the first century AD. Later wings were added—the plaster on the east wing was pink—and the house was finally abandoned around 380 AD. At first the houses were wooden bungalows with earth floors. More solid buildings developed from the second century onwards.

Roman towns used to be built along standard lines, not only with regard to their layout, but in their provision of public build-ings, designed to impress the local people, to develop in them a pride in their town and a realisation that they formed just one part of a great Empire which filled the known world. The centre of a Roman town was its market square or Forum with, on one side its town hall, or Basilica, while colonnades with shops stood on the other three sides. Canterbury's forum and basilica probably stood in the area of the modern County Hotel in the High Street, the public baths, with their bath rooms of different temperatures, their gymnasia, and their relaxation rooms, in modern St Margaret's Street. Here would congregate the citizens of Canter-bury, almost entirely British, for the Romans were content to govern by indirect rule and encourage a well-to-do native class to run the area's affairs. They must have taken to Roman ways quickly, for by the end of the first century an open air theatre was built which, with its oval bowl of banked earth or gravel on which were placed wooden seats, resembled the Roman theatre which can still be clearly seen at Verulamium (St Albans). A hundred years later this theatre was completely rebuilt. Between 210 and 220 AD a vast stone building was constructed,

33

open at the top, with a colonnade of arches encircling the banked seats on the outside. It was to stand for hundreds of years dominating the Roman city until its stones were finally dismantled after the Norman Conquest. Some of the great theatre's foundations can still be seen in the cellars of houses, at the southern side of St Margaret's Street. Once again there is an impression of a town of peace. Indeed the walls, which covered the same line as those of the medieval city, were not built until the end of the third century, when Saxon pirates were first attacking the south coast. For over 200 years Canterbury enjoyed a peace and a style of living—at least among the middle and upper classes—which must have seemed a fairy-tale world to those British farmers and labourers who were drawn into the county town to buy and exchange goods, or perhaps merely to gaze in wonder.

A visit to the Royal Museum at Canterbury, the museum at Richborough Castle, or the Maidstone Museum, can help us, with the aid of some historical imagination, to reconstruct life in the towns. One is struck immediately with the amount of coins displayed. Fifty thousand coins of the Roman period have been found at Richborough, many no doubt, intended for the pay parades of the occupation forces. At the 'Roman Pavement' house in Canterbury a hoard of coins was unearthed. A hoard was dug up near the Watling Street at Springhead, apparently tucked away by some traveller hurrying along the road before the final departures of the legions, who never returned for his treasure. Here is the most completely moneyed society yet known in Kent, a society rotted by inflation towards the end of the period, when the currency was being repeatedly depreciated. At this time tiny coins were in circulation, about 50 of which could be placed on an old-fashioned halfpenny.

Pottery abounds, much of it red glazed—beakers, jars, a strange barrel-shaped vessel, jugs. There are also two-handled wine jars, glass flagons, bangles, bottles, and a glass bowl. There are tiny little oil lamps, which must have been used as night lights and burial urns. The Romans buried their dead both by inhumation and cremation. There is a fine display at Richborough of women's make-up articles: a plated bronze mirror, combs, and glass phials for ointments, or cosmetics. A manicure set includes not only tweezers and nail-cleaners, but ear scoops for extracting wax. There are brooches, and finger rings of bronze, silver or gold. Whitstable oysters were already popular, judging from the remains. Bone was used for making needles, combs, and bodkins. Shale from Dorset and jet from Whitby have been made into bracelets and pendants. There is evidence of gambling, and at Richborough a marble slab has been incised as a gaming board, with dice made of bone, a dice box, and counters of bone and pottery. Men wrote either with a stylus or a wax board, or with ink (from an ink-well with an 'anti-spill' rim) on parchment.

One of the most impressive indications of Roman technical skill was the road system which the Romans quickly constructed not only, one suspects, for military or commercial purposes, but also to open up the country. They were to stand for many hundreds of years after the Roman troops left, and provide the line still for some modern roads, such as Watling Street (A2) or the strikingly straight Stone Street, the modern Canterbury-to-Hythe road. The roads were banked above the surrounding countryside, and their surface was made of crushed stones or gravel. They were cambered, so that water could drain away, and averaged around eight yards in width. Apart from Watling Street, with its feeder roads from the coast to Canterbury already referred to, the Romans built roads from Rochester and London which crossed areas which had scarcely previously been penetrated. One road ran south from Rochester to Maidstone. A few miles south-east of the latter it branched in two, one arm continuing due south straight across the Wealden forest till it reached the sea at Hastings, another cutting east on the high ridge near Sutton Valence and running south of Ashford to Lympne. Another road was built from the ironworking areas of the Weald to run through Tenterden and Ashford and over Godmersham Downs to Canterbury. From London the road to Lewes, later to form in part the western border of the county, linked London to the Wealden iron works and passed not far from the villa at Keston. But it was the Watling Street running due west from Canterbury to Rochester along the edge of Blean Forest which carried the greatest volume of traffic, both military and commercial, travelling to and from the continent. Along the road a number of minor towns and settlements grew up, among which Rochester and Springhead near Gravesend have been carefully excavated.

Rochester, like Canterbury, was walled in Roman times, though it was considerably smaller. The road crossed the Medway on a bridge at this point, and a Romano-British settlement developed around the crossing. The site was suitably dry for settlement, the soil here being chalk and gravel, while it was easy to defend being surrounded on three sides by marshes or the river itself. At Springhead, near Gravesend, a 25-acre settlement grew up at the junction of a navigable creek and Watling Street. It was probably a posting station for changing horses, where travellers could stay for a night before going on their way to London,

16   *The Forts of the Saxon shore (from Notitia Dignitatum MS, Bodleian Library, Oxford)*

and a small port. At first the buildings were, as usual, wooden with wattle-and-daub walls, but by 90 AD the first stone buildings had been built. Excavation has revealed a large public bakery, where grain was stored, ground, baked and sold—all in the same building. In addition, two corn-drying kilns have been found, where wheat was dried to make milling easier, or to prevent germination arising from the storing of wet corn. But it seems to have been as a religious centre, possessing at least six temples, that Springhead was best known.

The first temple was built before the end of the first century; later more were added. They were built near springs, in the manner of Romano-British worship, for it was usual to worship natural phenomena, especially sources of water. When several temples were built it was a sign that the site was held in very high esteem, and only a few sited either in Britain or in France, where remains of temples have also been found near springs, can show as many as six temples. The best-preserved temple was used until its destruction in 367 AD.

Believers' votive offerings have been found: 'If a devotee had something wrong with him . . . a model of the afflicted part of the body, or bronze letters making up a name, would be nailed to the walls, so that the gods would know what to cure. We actually found a nail still in the wall, and nearby a model of a thumb, arm and a letter "A".'[1] Another temple, with gaudily painted plaster, contained the remains of four children, while 14 more were buried nearby. It seems that they died in the terrible plague of 167 AD, when one third of the Roman Empire's population is reported to have perished. In 367 AD the idols in the best-preserved temple were thrown aside, and the building taken over by a blacksmith. It seems possible that the overthrow was a sign of Christian triumph. Life in Springhead continued after the departure of the last Roman soldiers, and the town was not apparently sacked. In between 425 and 450 AD the town was deserted, however, and the temples, bakery, and corn-drying kilns were left unused.

Roman troops were concentrated, as we have already seen, in a few forts—Richborough, Reculver, Dover, and Lympne. These forts, however, were not only filled with the military and civil servants. They naturally attracted to them a civilian population which lived by serving the occupation forces. At Richborough a supply base, with granaries and hastily constructed wooden

[1] W. S. Penn, 'The Roman Towns of Springhead', *Gravesend Historical Society*.

17   Pharos Lighthouse at Dover

buildings, protected by deep ditches and a wooden stockade, was quickly thrown up by the invaders. In 85 AD a great monument was built to mark the final conquest of Britain. 'It was faced with marble, with marble pillars and bronze statues, which towered above the sea, giving ships passing up the Wantsum a thrilling reminder of the might of Rome.'[2] During the next century settlement was mainly civilian, but about 280 AD a new strong fort, built as part of the national chain of coastal defences against continental raiders known as the forts of the Saxon shore, was erected. Some of the great stone walls still stand from that time; within them the monument was now being used merely as a look-out post.

At the other end of the Wantsum Channel the Romans quickly built a fortlet at Reculver, which stood then three quarters of a mile from the shore on a hill overlooking a good anchorage, like Richborough. After the conquest it was abandoned for 150 years. At the beginning of the third century a large fort, the first in the Saxon shore series, was built. The garrison was finally withdrawn around 360 AD. On the edge of the modern Romney Marsh the remains of the Roman fort at Lympne can still clearly be seen, littered down the hillside below Lympne Castle. It too began life as a fort by a harbour where the Channel fleet rode at anchor,

[2] J. P. Bushe-Fox, *Richborough Castle, Kent*.

and was later to be turned into one more base in the Saxon shore chain. Recent discoveries at Dover have revealed even more clearly how the use of Roman coastal bases changed during the period of their occupation.

The Pharos lighthouse, surprisingly intact, stands today in the grounds of Dover Castle. The light which was cast over the Channel came from great bonfires within the lighthouse, kept burning through the night. On the other side of the bay the remains of the second Roman lighthouse can still be seen on the western heights.

One of the most exciting recent excavations was that of the 'painted house'. A set of three big rooms, which must have formed part of a larger building, was found, together with the heating system, which has survived intact. The house is second century and its walls are covered with painted plaster in brilliant colours. The rooms may have been used as living rooms, or possibly they formed a shrine. 'In either case the Dover painted house provides exciting new evidence that the culture of Roman Britain, far from being that of a remote provincial backwater, was closely linked with the culture of Mediterranean lands and that foreign artists from the south were probably imported to decorate the homes of this country's wealthier inhabitants in Roman times.'[3]

We have already seen various signs of industrial activity in Roman Kent. At Darenth there was a large-scale fulling, and probably also a dyeing establishment attached to the villa. Loomweights, bobbins, and combs made of bone have been found on various Kent villas, while at Richborough there is evidence of spinning and weaving. Pottery was made in plenty, around Canterbury, on the Medway marshes near Upchurch and Lower Halstow, and not far from Springhead. Iron ore was dug from the Weald, where timber was also cut. Ragstone for the shore forts and for the walls at Canterbury and Rochester as well as London came from quarries near Lympne. There was a considerable demand for bricks and tiles, the centres of whose manufactures lay along the north-Kent coast and in the Medway valley. The miracle seems, on reflection, not so much that all this advanced activity was started in Roman Kent, but that it ended as completely as it did. It was of the essence of Roman colonisation, as we have seen, that the local population be trained to execute Roman techniques and that they should become completely involved in the administration of the country's affairs. And yet

[3] Professor Toynbee, *Kent Archaeological Review*, Autumn 1972.

all along one has had the feeling of a civilisation which was largely a façade. If times became hard, the conquerors divided among themselves, the army over-extended and, above all, the attacks from outside enemies were continuous and heavy, it was always likely that the British would return to a more barbarous pre-Conquest life.

Such attacks grew stronger in the fourth century. Picts from Scotland and Irish raiders advanced across the Thames. Saxon and Frankish raiders attacked the coast and penetrated deep into the county. Roman generals fought amongst each other, and there were various mutinies in the armies of occupation. In 367 AD the Romans were badly defeated and the following year the Emperor sent Count Theodosius to restore control. On his way from Richborough to London he saw robber gangs looting the countryside—and by no means all of these were foreign raiders. Many must have consisted of deserters from the army, or British peasants, or escaped slaves and debtors. Though Theodosius was successful, society was slowly disintegrating. Town life had been running down for a long time all over the Empire, and villas were being deserted. About 410 AD the Romans finally left, though over 30 years later a collection of Romano-British local authorities issued an appeal to Rome for help—which was ignored. Individual groups continued to try and live in the old ways, but it became more and more difficult to do so.

3
Anglo-Saxon Kent

Too much can be made of the final Roman departure from Kent around the year 410. Long before the last Roman soldiers were withdrawn, as we have seen, the Roman system of occupation and settlement had been disintegrating. There had never been many of them stationed in the county in any case, though their final withdrawal ended the military traffic along Watling Street and took from Rochester, Springhead, Canterbury and Richborough one of the main reasons for their existence. The Romano-British left behind had been fending for themselves for far longer than they could remember.

Nevertheless, life in the county was profoundly and irretrievably altered. Despite its earlier Christianisation, England was now regarded by Christian Europe as pagan. Many of the villas may have been looted, but most of their buildings still stood and the lines of their estates must still have been apparent. It seems surprising that the British made so little effort to continue a way of life with which they were deeply familiar, but no such attempt was made, and Lullingstone was left a ruin. The wall around Canterbury stood for hundreds of years, until the builders of the medieval town constructed their own defences on precisely the same circuit. Augustine's missionaries may have used its stones and bonding tiles for the construction of their churches, but otherwise it served no purpose. The great theatre—one of the works of the giants, as the new invaders called them—continued to dominate Canterbury and its shell was still standing at the Norman Conquest. But the life of the Roman system was slowly slipping away, and nothing was found to revive it.

By about the year 450 England was dominated by native chiefs whose spheres of influence fluctuated from year to year. Kent formed part of the territory of a Welsh King, Vortigern, whose people lived along the old Roman frontier between England and Wales, were half romanised, and had been trained by the Romans to provide for the frontier's defence. It seems that Vortigern, faced with the old problem of Saxon raiders, and unable to defend his lands, decided to ask these poachers to become gamekeepers, as the Romans had done with his predecessors. This is how Bede, whose account is very similar to that found in the *Anglo-Saxon Chronicle*, describes the famous invitation: 'At that time the race of the Angles or Saxons, invited by Vortigern, came to Britain in three warships and by his command were granted a place of settlement in the eastern part of the island, ostensibly to fight on behalf of the country, but their real intention was to conquer it.'

The Chronicle specifically mentions Ebbsfleet, on Thanet, as the place of landing. Bede continues: 'First they fought against the enemy who attacked from the north and the Saxons won the victory. A report of this as well as of the fertility of the island and the slackness of the Britons reached their homes and at once a much larger fleet was sent over with a stronger band of warriors; this, added to the contingent already there, made an invincible army. The newcomers received from the Britons a grant of land in their midst on condition that they fought against their foes for the peace and safety of the country, and for this the soldiers were also to receive pay. They came from three very powerful Germanic tribes, the Saxons, Angles, and Jutes. The people of Kent and the inhabitants of the Isle of Wight are of Jutish origin.'

Soon the new colonists, whose leaders were two brothers Hengist and Horsa, seem to have rounded on their hosts. The *Anglo-Saxon Chronicle* records events as follows: '455. In this year Hengest and Horsa fought against King Vortigern at the place which is called Ægelesthrep (Aylesford) and his brother Horsa was killed there; and after that Hengest and his son Æsc succeeded to the Kingdom.

456 (or 457 in one version). In this year Hengest and his son Æsc fought against the Britons in the place which is called Creacanford (? Crayford) and killed four thousand men; and the Britons then deserted Kent and fled with great fear to London.'[1] Yet another army of colonists had arrived and settled.

The new men did not call themselves Jutes (though from now

[1] The translations quoted are from *Bede's Ecclesiastical History* edited by Cosgrave and Mynors (Oxford 1969) and *The Anglo-Saxon Chronicle* edited by Dorothy Whitelock (Eyre and Spottiswoode, 1961).

on, to avoid confusion, I shall do so) and did not come from Jutland. After they had settled they refer to themselves as 'Kentings', men living in Kent. They seem to have been a Frankish people, living on the middle Rhine, who wandered down the river to its mouth. Here they mixed with other peoples coming in particular from northern Holland (Frisia) and crossed the North Sea to Kent. Our extremely scanty knowledge of their origins is based partly on the similarity between their pottery and jewellery and that found in the Rhine valley and Frisia, and partly on similarities of place-names. Place-name evidence again provides us with our knowledge of their areas of settlement in Kent, coupled with excavation of their burial sites.

There were not many of these fighting farmers—perhaps 25,000—in the county. They lived chiefly in the countryside in small groups of about 50 people, though they did not shun town life, for there appears to be no break in Canterbury's occupation and they had settlements at Sarre, Fordwich, and Dover. They settled chiefly in east Kent, east of Canterbury where the land was easiest to work, but also along Watling Street and, like their prehistoric forerunners, in the Medway and Darent valleys. Not

18 Sixth Century silver-gilt brooches set with garnets. From a noble woman's grave at Lyminge

one of their burial places has been found in the Weald, in Romney Marsh, or along the north-Kent coast from Sheppey to the Isle of Thanet, nor is there one single place-name of early Saxon origin in those areas. The men, like the Celtic tribes before the long Roman occupation, were warriors and hunters, and farmed simply, whilst the women wove and spun.

A visit to the Royal Museum at Canterbury or to the Maidstone Museum will quickly reveal the skill of many Jutish craftsmen. Here may be seen the jewels, the pottery, the fighting implements, and the glasswork with which the men and women were buried, presumably because it was believed that they would prove helpful in the world to come. There are bronze bowls, brooches, and bangles. A radiate headed brooch from Lyminge set with garnets, the arms going out like the rays of the sun, is particularly impressive. There are beads of amber (especially popular),

44

glass, and baked clay, while the amethyst beads of Westbere and Sarre stand out from their case at Canterbury Museum. Garnets are to be found in large numbers; they were imported, but seem probably to have been set by local craftsmen. There are glass vases of the fifth to seventh centuries, along with glass beakers, cups, bottles and jars. Much of the glasswork was imported from the Rhineland and northern France, but some may well have been manufactured in Kent. Nearly a quarter of the glass found in Britain during this period has come from Faversham, and it seems likely that the area became a centre of manufacture. Iron swords, axeheads, arrowheads, and knives are to be seen in plenty, as one would expect.

The contents of two graves in particular are worth enumerating. At Lyminge, where the cemetery was used from the second half

20   The Finglesham Buckle, 7th century

of the fifth century until the third quarter of the sixth, there has been excavated the grave of a lady of clearly superior status. She was buried with two silver brooches set with garnets, other silver squareheaded brooches, gold braid used to decorate a head band, and a perforated silver spoon, with a crystal ball under the bowl. At Sarre around the year 575, another wealthy lady was buried whose possessions included a glass bell-beaker, six gold bracelets, a crystal ball in a mount, several brooches set with garnets, a silver wire ring, amber beads, gold braid and a weaving batten. These discoveries would indicate considerable differences in rank, and do much to alter our impression of the Jutish settlers as ignorant isolated smallholders.

As for the British, their fate must have varied. Some were killed, many fled—to the south-west of England, to Wales and to the forest of the Weald, or Andresweald, as it was now called. Many became serfs, or slaves, of the Jutes. The old English word *walh* or *wealh* means both Briton and serf. From it derives Walmer— the sea coast of the Britons—and Wales itself. Some probably stayed on in the county, living on the high lands, and leaving the valleys to the invaders, as their forefathers had left them to the Romans. Once again one has the feeling of a persistent British submerged life, of which one has only rare glimpses, but which has persisted since the Iron-Age. The life of the settlers was little influenced by them, and few British words entered the English language.

For 130 years after the Jutish settlement there are no surviving written records. But in the second half of the sixth century both Bede and the *Anglo-Saxon Chronicle* become specific, with the accession of Ethelbert, as King of Kent. For Ethelbert seems to have been a great Bretwalda, or overlord, reigning over half of England, and Kent was both prosperous and powerful compared with the rest of the country.

He was in regular contact with the continent, and had married Bertha, the daughter of Charibert, King of Paris. She was a Christian and, according to Bede: 'Ethelbert had received her from her parents on condition that she should be allowed to practise her faith and religion unhindered, with a bishop named Liudhard whom they had provided for her to support her faith.' Once again, Kent was to be influenced, overpowered even, by forces from the Continent of Europe.

The missionary expedition, led by Saint Augustine, which was to convert, or rather to reconvert, southern England to Christianity had been planned by Pope Gregory I well in advance. Before he became Pope, according to Bede, Gregory had unsuccessfully urged on his predecessor the sending of a mission to Britain, and had offered to lead it himself. In 595 there is recorded a letter from Gregory to a priest, Candidus, instructing him to buy Anglo-Saxon slave boys. Gregory's plan was that the boys would be trained in Italian monasteries to become missionaries to their own people. The next year a mission of monks set out headed by Augustine, Provost of St Andrew's Monastery on the Caelian Hill at Rome, where Gregory himself had been trained. Their understandable reluctance to proceed with their dangerous expedition is described by Bede who relies, throughout his account of the mission, on information gained from the records of St Augustine's Abbey; Canterbury: 'In the fourteenth year of this emperor (Maurice) and about 150 years after the coming of the Angles to Britain, Gregory, prompted by divine inspiration, sent a servant of God named Augustine and several more God-fearing monks with him to preach the word of God to the English race. In obedience to the Pope's commands, they undertook this task and had already gone a little way on their journey when they were paralysed with terror. They began to contemplate returning home rather than going to a barbarous, fierce, and unbelieving nation whose language they did not even understand.'

Augustine was sent back to the Pope to ask his permission 'to give up so dangerous, wearisome and uncertain a journey.' Gregory sent the party a letter dated 23 July 596, which convinced them that they must persevere and which was preserved by Augustine and his successors at Canterbury:

'Gregory, servant of the servants of God, to the servants of our Lord.

My dearly beloved sons, it would have been better not to have undertaken a noble task, then to turn back deliberately from what you have begun: so it is right that you should carry out with all diligence this good work which you have begun with the help of the Lord. Therefore do not let the toilsome journey nor the tongues of evil speakers deter you. But carry out the task you have begun under the guidance of God with all constancy and fervour. Be sure that, however great your task may be, the glory of your eternal

47

reward will be still greater. When Augustine your prior returns, now, by our appointment, your abbot, humbly obey him in all things, knowing that whatever you do under his direction will be in all respects profitable to your souls. May Almighty God protect you by His grace and grant that I may see the fruit of your labours in our heavenly home. Though I cannot labour with you, yet because I should have been glad indeed to do so, I hope to share in the joy of your reward. May God keep you safe, my dearly loved sons.'

The party, which contained about 40 men, recruited some Frankish interpreters and landed in Thanet, probably at Ebbsfleet. Here they stayed, and Augustine sent a message to Ethelbert, telling him that 'he had come from Rome bearing the best of news, namely the sure and certain promise of eternal joys in heaven and an endless kingdom with the living and true God to those who received it.'

After a while Ethelbert came to see for himself what the visitors were like, and to hear what they had to say. The two sides sat in the open air, where the Christians would not be able to get the better of the King and his men through any magical arts. Augustine and his monks carried a silver cross and a picture of Christ painted on wood. Their message had an effect on Ethelbert, though it did not yet convince him: 'Then he said to them: "The words and the promises you bring are fair enough, but because they are new to us and doubtful, I cannot consent to accept them and forsake those beliefs which I and the whole English race have held so long. But as you have come on a long pilgrimage and are anxious, I perceive, to share with us things which you believe to be true and good, we do not wish to do you harm, on the contrary, we will receive you hospitably and provide what is necessary for your support; nor do we forbid you to win all you can to your faith and religion by your preaching." So he gave them a dwelling in the city of Canterbury, which was the chief city of all his dominions; and in accordance with his promise, he granted them provisions and did not refuse them freedom to preach. It is related that as they approached the city in accordance with their custom carrying the holy cross and the image of our great King and Lord, Jesus Christ, they sang this litany in unison: "We beseech thee, O Lord, in thy great mercy, that Thy wrath and anger may be turned away from this city and from Thy holy house, for we have sinned. Alleluia." '

Kent was used to invaders. But no previous invader had spoken or behaved in any way like this.

Augustine found that in one place, at least, Christian worship was being regularly offered. To the east of the city, outside the Roman wall, there still stands today the little church of Saint Martin's, one of the oldest churches in Europe. Queen Bertha with her chaplain had been worshipping here and the building was probably constructed after her arrival in England. Here Augustine and his monks 'began to meet to chant the psalms, to pray, to say mass, to preach, and to baptize until, when the king had been converted to the faith [this occurred in 601] they received greater liberty to preach everywhere and to build or restore churches.' At the same time they began to construct, fairly quickly, a base in an old church, built in Roman times, which Ethelbert gave them, along with 'possessions of various kinds for their needs.' This church must have stood where the Cathedral now stands, though no traces of a Roman building have been found. It was here that the first monastery of Christ Church was built.

From the beginning the methods of the missionaries were very different from those which we, unconsciously perhaps basing our expectations on a pattern of nineteenth-century missionary work in Africa, have learned to expect. There seem to have been no field preaching tours, no militant attempt to bring the church to the people. Quite the reverse in fact; Augustine established his church with royal help, surrounded it with a stockade or hedge, and built up his Christian community. '. . . in all things they practised what they preached and kept themselves prepared to endure adversities even to the point of dying for the truths they proclaimed'.

When, after a while, Augustine sent for help to the Pope the latter sent not only missionaries but 'all such things as were generally necessary for the worship and ministry of the church, such as sacred vessels, altar cloths, and church ornaments, vestments for priests and clerks, relics of the holy apostles and martyrs, and very many manuscripts'.

The monastery—or 'minster'—and not the parish church was to be the centre of Christian penetration, and was to remain so until the time of the Danish invasions. As the church expanded in Kent more minsters were built, and the pattern of monastic missionary work continued. This is one of the reasons why for many years the tribal Saxon religion continued alongside the new beliefs. Unless he lived near a monastery the Saxon peasant was probably unaware of the Christian Church's existence.

Some years after Augustine had secured his base in Canterbury the King gave him further land, outside the city wall, between the Cathedral and St Martin's Church, and here he established the Benedictine abbey of SS Peter and Paul, where he, Bertha, and Ethelbert were to be buried, along with succeeding archbishops and kings. It was later renamed St Augustine's Abbey. Soon Augustine had consecrated another Kentish bishop, Justus, to the diocese of Rochester. His church, like that of the monastery from which both Pope Gregory and Saint Augustine had gone into the world, was named after Saint Andrew, and a Benedictine priory was attached to it. At Lyminge a minster was founded for Ethelbert's daughter Ethelburga, and much of Romney Marsh belonged to it. There were minsters at the channel ports of Dover and Folkestone, while at Reculver King Egbert founded a minster for his mass priest, where clergy were trained. Two other great minsters were founded, at Minster-in-Sheppey and Minster-in-Thanet. The Sheppey foundation was the work of an East-Anglian princess who had married King Earconberht of Kent, and marked the Thames passage from Kent to her native land with her minster. It is thought that Minster-in-Thanet may have been founded by her son King Egbert, who gave land to his sister, who built the church and became the first abbess. The next was her daughter Mildred who became the second Kentish saint after Augustine. The abbey, like most of the Kentish minsters, suffered terribly at the hands of the Vikings, who slaughtered the abbess and her nuns in a raid of 797 and finally forced it to close down.

We can imagine the Saxon peasant, drawn to the minster enclosure, standing peering over the stockade on a Sunday or a saint's day. If he went inside the church, which would be the most solidly constructed building he had encountered, his eyes would be drawn to the altar where the priest, dressed in golden vestments, would be speaking a strange language, and other clergy would be chanting. He would watch for the moment of climax, when the priest would bless the white bread of sacrifice, and the congregation bow down before a new and more effective idol than those provided by their traditional gods. Earlier he would have seen the procession of clergy from the altar to the front of the congregation for the reading of the gospel, and seen that the gospel book was treated with a reverence due to Christ Himself. The candles would be bright in the gloom, and the atmosphere heavy with incense. The gospel might be followed by a sermon, whose object would be to interpret the passage of Scripture which was read. This was the only part of the service which might be spoken in English though we cannot be certain even of that. The offertory would be taken in kind, and the people's gifts—bread, oil or wine —collected by the priest in a basket. After the service the congregation would return to their ordinary lives, passing the little houses of the monks as they left the enclosure. They would be back again, if not next Sunday, the Sunday afterwards. But the process of penetration was a slow one. Saxon gods, probably even, among the British, pre-Roman gods continued to be worshipped for many years. The county's history, though once again radically altered, changed almost imperceptibly, if looked at in terms of one or two generations.

The Saxons used to hold feasts after the autumn slaughter of beasts. What else could be done with the animals except eat a large number of them, for they could not be fed through the winter? The Christians used to feast too at this time which they conveniently named as the birthday of Christ. Still at the Yule feast—the very name was carried into the Christian era—the men would dress in animal skins and in the masks of animals, capering for hours in the firelight, throwing fantastic shadows, to induce good hunting in the months ahead. The veneration which was paid to the sanctuaries was transferred to the churches, where many of the images of the saints and of the holy family must have looked very much like the old idols. The feeling that evil was all about, and particularly in forests and storms, was carried deep into Christian times. The *Anglo-Saxon Chronicle*, which was written by monks, recorded the presence of fiery dragons flying in the air of Northumbria when the Vikings first appeared off the coast. If holy wells, incantations and amulets protected the colonist Jute from the evil which could strike him down at any moment, holy water, prayers, saints' relics, and crucifixes served a similar purpose to his devout successor at the time of Alfred. But the Church fought bitterly against many superstitions, against the belief, for instance, that after a death in a house, grain must be burned to ensure the health of the living, or that girls could be cured of fever by being placed in an oven. It tried to prevent the docking of horses' tails, for the people were convinced that elves would otherwise cling to the tails and drive the poor beasts round and round in the night so that they would be unable to work the next morning. Yet the Church seems to have been happy to adopt the form of an ancient Anglo-Saxon marriage service virtually word for word. The bride's contract ran as follows: 'I take thee, John, to be my wedded husband, to have and to hold from this day forward, for better for worse, for richer and poorer, in sickness

21 *St Augustine's Abbey, Canterbury just before its dissolution*

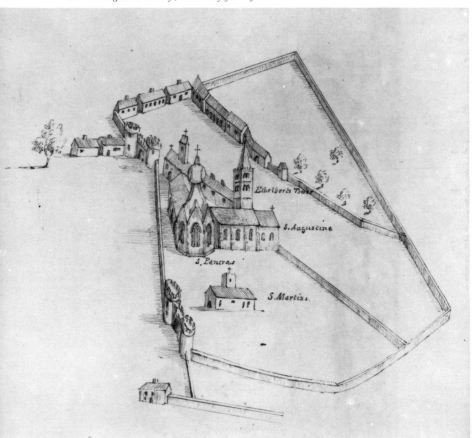

and health, to be bonny and buxom, in bed and at board, till death do us part, and thereto I plight thee my troth.'

Until the end of the eighth century Kent remained an independent kingdom. The county then was conquered by King Offa of Mercia (757–96), who controlled all territories south of the Humber, and east of the Wessex border with Sussex. Offa was the first man to use the title 'King of the English' and was addressed by the Pope as *Rex Anglorum*. He took over the Canterbury mint and struck a considerable number of pennies, many of which have survived. After his death Kent rebelled, and though the rebellion was suppressed, the connection with Mercia remained unpopular. In 825 King Egbert of Wessex decisively defeated the Mercians, and received the submission of Kent, Surrey, and Sussex. From now on the lands south of the Thames were unified into the Kingdom of Wessex, and the county ceases to have an independent history, so that its story becomes even more a reflection of the whole nation's history.

The impact of attacks from the next succession of invaders, the Danes, which was so considerable in northern and eastern England was not so great in Kent, for this time the foreigners did not settle. Kent never became part of the 'Danelaw', and the raiders eventually moved away. But the effect on those parts of the county which suffered from their ferocity must have been traumatic, even if Danish colonisation was to be concentrated north of the

22   *East Kent at the time of the Danish invasions*

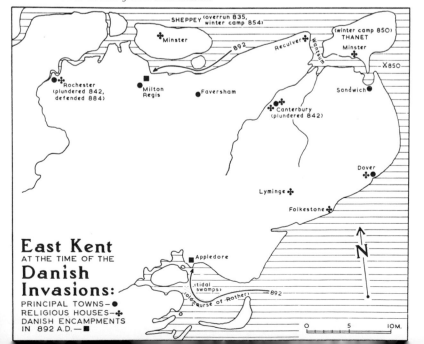

SHEPPEY (overrun 835, winter camp 854)

Minster

892

Reculver

(winter camp 850) THANET

Minster

X850

Rochester (plundered 842, defended 884)

Milton Regis

Faversham

Sandwich

Canterbury (plundered 842)

Dover

Lyminge

Folkestone

East Kent
AT THE TIME OF THE
Danish
Invasions:
PRINCIPAL TOWNS – ●
RELIGIOUS HOUSES – ✠
DANISH ENCAMPMENTS
IN 892 A.D. – ■

Appledore

(tidal swamps)

old course of Rother

892

N

0   5   10M.

Thames.

The first reference to Danish attacks on Kent in the *Anglo-Saxon Chronicle* is a laconic one, and refers to the year 835: 'In this year heathen men ravaged Sheppey.'

From that time onwards the islands of Sheppey and Thanet, with their rich and undefended monasteries, lying so close to the shore, were to provide a regular and convenient target for Viking raids. From the 850s the attackers were to winter on the islands, resuming their inland raids in the spring. The great halls of the minsters at Thanet and at Sheppey were used as feasting rooms or general headquarters by the Danes, who were said to have angrily refused any offer of salt meat from the local people, even at the height of winter. So the farmers were made to slaughter their breeding herds, and the whole economy of farm life was destroyed, for often the Danes took the seed corn too. At anchor in the Wantsum rode the famous long-ships, with their fantastic prows of carved painted dragons' heads, snakes, or sea monsters. The Northmen had raided deep inland, as far as the Medway, and had burnt Rochester, along with many farmsteads which had proved resistant to their wishes. There was no reason to think that they would ever go away for long, though already the Kentings were taking to the futile practice of paying money to the invaders, to persuade them to try their luck elsewhere.

'865. In this year the heathen army encamped on Thanet and made peace with the people of Kent. And the people of Kent promised them money for that peace. And under cover of that peace and promise of money the army stole away inland by night and ravaged all eastern Kent.' (Records the *Anglo-Saxon Chronicle*.)

The climax came in 892: 'In this year the great Danish army . . . went westward to Boulogne, and they were provided with ships there, so that they crossed in one journey, horses and all, and then came up into the estuary of the Lympne* with 200 ships. That estuary is in east Kent, and at the east end of that great wood which we call Andred. The wood is from east to west 120 miles long, or longer, and 30 miles broad. The river . . . comes out of the Weald. They rowed their ships up the river as far as the Weald, four miles from the mouth of the estuary, and there they stormed a fortress . . . Then immediately afterwards Haesten came with 80 ships up the Thames estuary and made himself a fortress at Milton and the other army made one at Appledore.'†

* The river Lympne—or Limen—is the river Rother. It has changed its course since those days and the whole coastline has altered.

† In 892 Appledore was close to the coast.

But Kent now had a powerful defender in Alfred, King of Wessex. The next year he advanced to a point in the centre of Kent half way between the two Danish armies. The Danes escaped from the Weald, travelling 'in small bands and mounted companies, by whatever side it was then undefended by the English Army.' Haesten also went north and crossed the Thames. For the next 100 years Kent was free of attacks, though Kentishmen were fighting for a while as part of the Wessex army against the invaders, until the Danes made peace with Wessex, and settled down to cultivate the eastern and northern part of England which was now theirs.

The familiar pattern of payment followed by renewed ravagings recurred. The climax came between 1009 and 1012.

In 1009 'there came . . . after Lammas (1 August) the immense raiding army which we called Thorkel's army to Sandwich and immediately turned their course to Canterbury and would quickly have captured the borough if the citizens had not still more quickly asked them for peace. And all the people of east Kent made peace with that army and gave them 3,000 pounds.' After Martinmas (11 November) they returned to Kent, took up winter quarters on the Thames, and attacked London. During the next year the Danish army attacked south-eastern and central England. The English were divided, dilatory and cowardly and could offer little resistance. In 1011 the Danes turned back to Canterbury, and entered the city through treachery, capturing Alphege, Archbishop of Canterbury, the Bishop of Rochester, the Abbess of St Mildred's Thanet, and others, burnt the town and the Cathedral, and returned to their ships, taking the archbishop with them. Alphege refused to agree to ransom money, and was killed by the Danes at Greenwich: 'They were also very drunk, for wine from the south had been brought there. They seized the bishop, and brought him to their assembly on the eve of the Sunday of the octave of Easter, which was 19 April, and shamefully put him to death there: they pelted him with bones and with ox-heads and one of them struck him on the head with the back of an axe, that he sank down with the blow and his holy blood fell on the ground, and so he sent his holy soul to God's Kingdom.'

Twelve years later when Kent was under the control of Cnut, the Danish King, Alphege's body was brought back home 'with much glory and joy and songs of praise into Canterbury'. Cnut

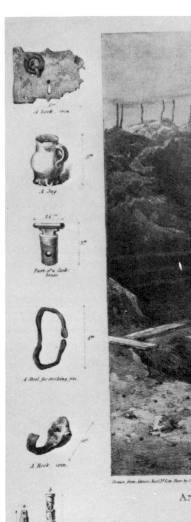

A Lock iron

A Jug

Part of a Cock brass

A Steel for stocking fire

A Hook iron

a A leaden octangular Plummet
b A leathern Ink horn

Drawn from Nature Acut. 3d Edtn Publ by J. B. Burdine

ANCIENT VESSEL DISCOVERED IN THE CHANNEL OF T

This Vessel which is supposed to be one of the Fleet abandoned by the Danes after their defeat in the reign of king the Great the Hold. She was found in a perfectly sound and entire state buried ten feet deep in the sand in the channel of the river Rother vessel. In clearing out the hold several utensils were found. The most interesting of which have been accurately copied two natural human skeletons and those of a goat, a dog, and a bear. This most interesting and extraordinary remnant of antiquity is in a high state of pre

London. Pub. by Kidwell and Rotter Row Lon.

Marks cut on a board 12th by 15th supposed to be a rough chart
of the Ships route. An inkstand was also found on the board

56

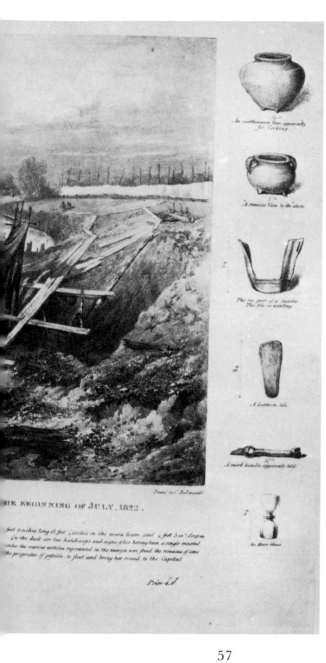

An earthenware Vase, apparently for Cooking

A similar Vase to the above

The toe part of a Sandal. The Side is wanting

A Leathern Sole

A sword handle apparently Gold

An Hour Glass

Printed by C Hullmandel

THE BEGINNING OF JULY, 1822.

feet 6 inches long 15 feet 3 inches in the main beam, and 4 feet 3 in. deep in
On the deck are two hatchways, and signs of her having been a single masted
under the various articles represented in the margin were found the remains of some
the proprietor, if possible, to float and bring her round to the Capital

Price 4.6.

23   A Danish vessel
discovered in the Rother
in 1822

himself, who had been converted to Christianity after a savage past, and who had completely restored the Cathedral, carried Alphege's body into Christ Church.

As we have seen, the Jutes settled chiefly in the areas which were already the most colonised: east Kent, and in the river valleys. But slowly, over many generations, the settlement of the county was extended, and by the time of the Norman Conquest large areas even of Romney Marsh and of the Weald had been cleared. Of the two the clearance of the Marsh was the more advanced. It has been reckoned that it supported a population of five people per square mile in the time of the Domesday Survey, compared to less than one in the Weald, and 17 in the most highly settled area of the county, that behind Folkestone.

The Romans, with their coastal base at Lympne, were the first to set about reclaiming the large area of coastal marshes lumped under the title Romney Marsh. It was said that they exhausted the local Marshmen with their banking, drainage, and clearance schemes. The Marsh was already being dignified by the name of province in the ninth century, and a strange reference in Nennius's *Catalogue of British Wonders*, written in the same period, gives us a glimpse, even if a rather mythical one, of how the clearance was proceeding: 'The first marvel is the Lommon (Limen) Marsh, for in it are 340 islands with men living on them. It is girt by 340 rocks, and in every rock is an eagle's nest, and 340 rivers flow into it; and there goes out of it into the sea but one river, which is called the Lemn (Limen).'

Very slowly the islands were being joined up, often under the supervision of the monks who owned so much of the land. By the time of the Domesday survey the hundreds of Romney Marsh had taken their medieval form, which would indicate a fair degree of settlement, while Romney was already well established as a fortified burgh and a port with long-standing privileges. There was extensive fishing at the mouth of the Limen and various salt works are recorded.

The penetration and clearing of the Wealden forest took hundreds of years to complete, and by the end of the Anglo-Saxon period the process was still at the pioneering stage. The Romans had mined iron ore in the Weald, and had driven roads through it but the Jutes left the great forest severely alone. They feared the spirits, as did the Danes. Probably some Britons lived there, or Welsh as they were called, whose forefathers had taken to the woods when the Jutes had moved into Kent. There would always have been outlaws or refugees of all sorts, treating the forest of Andred as colonial America treated the backwoods. It was not until the ninth century, to judge from place-name evidence, that Saxon clearing of the Weald began.

The Weald was cleared by what would appear to be a fairly orderly demarcation of the forest into areas belonging to manors in other parts of the county. Kentish manors to the north and east of the Weald were awarded substantial stretches of forest which they would use either for grazing swine or for wood. Swiss villagers in the valleys similarly use the mountains for wood or for summer pasture today. Such stretches were called denes or dens (the word means a woodland swine pasture) and the Weald is full of villages ending in -den, like Marden, Biddenden, or Bethersden. The dene was connected to the parent manor by a drove way. Thus the manor of Wye owned a Wealden area, a good 20 miles away, covering the modern parishes of Cranbrook and Hawkhurst, and Tenterden belonged to the men of Thanet. The manors of Swanscombe and Southfleet owned woodland at Tonbridge, and the royal manor of Milton, on the north Kent coast, regularly received 50 shillings from the men of the Weald.

In the midst of the dene would stand the compound, a clearing in the forest which would contain houses and pig-sties, defended by a wooden stockade, like Iron-Age settlements in earlier times. The herdsmen and foresters were far away from home, and so were forced to cultivate the clearings for the support of themselves and their families. Pigs are voracious destroyers of undergrowth, which made the process of felling easier. By such slow means was Andredesweald colonised, and though substantial sections of the forest remained untouched, by the time of the conquest other parts had been transformed. Twenty years after Hastings, Newenden, on the Kent-Sussex border, a Wealden village, was regularly holding its own market. The method of clearance has left its stamp on the modern topography of Wealden villages. They tend to be spaced apart fairly evenly and divided by about three miles of countryside.

The impression one gains from the very scanty evidence available of Kentish life during the centuries between the first Danish raids and the Norman settlement is that of an extremely simple agricultural life dominated by work, a life which would not have seemed outrageously strange to a Celtic man of Kent, living many centuries before the Romans. Their windowless houses made of wood, thatched, and with wattle-and-daub walls were larger, but seem to have been basically very similar. Physically they would probably have resembled those earlier Jutes, whose bones were found in a cemetery at Polehill, near Otford, excavated in 1967. Of 100 skeletons examined, one third were of children who had died before the age of 16. Another third died before they were 25, and most of the remainder did not live to 40. The men were between five foot six inches and six foot in height, the women between five foot two inches and five and a half feet. Like their prehistoric ancestors they were sufferers from osteoarthritis.

Their settlements were more like hamlets than traditional villages of the classic English type, a characteristic of Kent which was to continue into the middle ages. The three large open fields, divided into strips, where the villagers held their land and which they farmed to a large extent communally, were not known in Kent. A few houses would be grouped together in a little piece of ribbon development, and from them the farmers could go out to farm their own holdings. These would form a separate, a self-contained unit, measuring about 40 acres, and called a yoke or *jugum*, a measurement peculiar to Kent. Mr J. E. A. Jolliffe, in his researches into the Manor of Wye, has shown how its tenements were far-flung. They were 'dependent islands, surviving today as farmsteads. They occur at intervals spread over the modern parishes of Wye, Boughton Aluph, Godmersham, Crundale, Brook, Willesborough, Ashford, Kingsnothe, Servington, and Orlestone . . . each a rounded hamlet complete in its own fields and sufficient to itself.'[2] Onto this independent peasantry was later grafted the system of feudalism, but it was to prove an uneasy mixture in Kent. Always there was the assertion of independence, the claim that the Kentish yeomen was different.

> *A Knight of Cales,*
> *A nobleman of Wales,*
> *And a Laird of the north Countree ;*
> *A yeoman of Kent*
> *With his yearly rent*
> *Will buy them out all three.*

This fourteenth century poem was to have its basis in pre-feudal

[2] J. E. A. Jolliffe, *Pre-Feudal England: the Jutes*, p. 8.

Pictura et scriptura huius pagine subtus
uisa : est de propria manu scī Dunstani.

24 *St Dunstan at the
feet of Christ. From a
drawing in Dunstan's
own hand*

Kent. The distinctive Kentish inheritance law of gavel-kind, by
which land was split up among all a family's sons if the father died
intestate, obtained over the county before the Conquest and
accentuated the tendency towards the creation of independent
farms. So too did the large proportion of woodland in the county,
for farms cleared from forest land were always individually owned.

Already too, the church's position as a great landowner had
developed. Great tracts of the county belonged to the Archbishop,
the Bishop of Rochester, or to the two great Canterbury monasteries. In the villages many parish churches had now been built,
generally at the orders of a wealthy man or of the monks. Church
records at the time of Domesday show 150 parish churches, apart

from those mentioned in the Survey. Most of these were wooden buildings and have not survived, but a certain amount of Saxon stone church building has remained. St Martin's at Canterbury has a substantial Saxon element, as has St Mildred's Church in the same city. The Church of St Mary in Castro, built within the walls of Dover Castle around 1000, is unusually complete, despite Victorian reconstruction. All the churches would have had paintings on the wall of Jesus's life, especially of his miracles, of his birth and death, and of his resurrection, while the Last Judgment would have confronted the congregation with its warning of punishment to come. The church was no longer a long way away, in a foreign monastic enclosure; it was at hand, in the hamlet.

The monastery from the beginning was a centre of learning as well as evangelism. Archbishop Theodore and Abbot Hadrian brought Greek and Roman learning and a knowledge of Roman law to Canterbury, as well as a better knowledge of the scriptures. According to Bede, writing a generation later, Theodore and Hadrian: 'gathered a crowd of disciples . . . and together with the books of holy writ, they also taught them the arts of ecclesiastical poetry, astronomy and arithmetic. . . . There are still living at this day some of their scholars who are as well versed in the Greek and Latin tongues as in their own.'

Later, in the middle of the eighth century, Canterbury was producing fine illuminated manuscripts, three of which have survived. Later again under Archbishop Dunstan (who was Archbishop of Canterbury from 960 to 988) Canterbury saw a monastic revival. Dunstan, like so many of his successors, was primarily concerned to improve the quality of his clergy. He set out to reform the monasteries where many of the clergy were trained and which had often fallen into lay hands, with their abbacies passing by hereditary right. His monks became bishops, or heads of other monasteries, and the whole quality of the church's life was transformed. Like Theodore, he was a learned man, who, it was said, possessed a good knowledge not only of the Scriptures and of manuscripts, of the liberal arts, and of the church chants, but also of the 'mechanical arts', of the work of the blacksmith who manufactured horse shoes, ploughshares, and bolts, and of the gold and silver smith, who made church vessels, especially communion cups and altar ornaments, rings or brooches.

4
Medieval Kent

William of Normandy's conquest of England was achieved with surprising ease. After his victory at Battle, inland from Hastings, in 1066 the invaders encountered little organised resistance. William did not march straight for London, which would have meant cutting across the Weald, but wisely preferred to avoid a route which would have provided such easy opportunities for ambush. He turned east along the coast, burnt and plundered Romney, which had earlier resisted Norman attack, and moved on Dover, which capitulated without a fight. Against the Conqueror's wishes, some of his followers set fire to a group of houses and the whole town was nearly destroyed. William stayed in Dover for a week or so, and improved the fortifications. Dysentery broke out among his troops and when he moved inland to Canterbury, the sick were left behind under the care of a garrison. Along the Dover road he was met, according to his chaplain, by the men of Kent, who swore an oath of loyalty to him, and gave him hostages. From Canterbury William made for London and eventually, 10 weeks after Hastings, he was crowned in Westminster Abbey on Christmas Day, 1066. The next year, when William was in Normandy, and his half-brother Odo, Bishop of Bayeux, who had been made Earl of Kent, in charge of the county, a plan was formed by a group of Kentishmen. The dissident Eustace of Boulogne was to bring a strong force across the Straits, join up with the Kentishmen, and attack Dover, while Bishop Odo was in the north. News of the plan leaked out, and the Dover garrison was waiting for Eustace and his men when they landed. They were driven back to their ships in confusion, and the English force dispersed before it was properly assembled. From

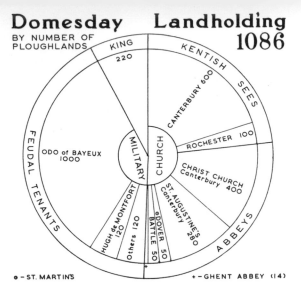

KING
220

KENTISH SEES

CANTERBURY 600

ROCHESTER 100

FEUDAL TENANTS

ODO of BAYEUX
1000

MILITARY

CHURCH

CHRIST CHURCH
Canterbury 400

ST AUGUSTINE'S
Canterbury

HUGH de MONTFORT
120

Others 120

BATTLE 50

●DOVER 50

ST AUGUSTINE'S
280

ABBEYS

● - ST. MARTIN'S

+ - GHENT ABBEY (14)

25   *The ownership of land in 1086*

now on there was no organised resistance to the new colonists.

The Normans set about their military occupation and civil administration of England with an efficiency which is reminiscent of the Romans, and Kent was one of the first counties to be settled. The Domesday Survey, which was completed at William's orders in 18 months from 1085–6, when taken alongside contemporary church surveys, provides us with a detailed picture of the county with which we have not previously been presented. It is true that naturally each record regards the county from the point of view of its own masters and is consequently partial. Domesday is compiled so that the King can know what taxes and what soldiers the county is capable of contributing, and what royal lands he holds. The Church surveys consist of *The Excerpta*, a catalogue of lands held by St Augustine's Abbey, the *Textus Roffensis*, a list of churches belonging to the Bishop of Rochester, and *The Domesday Monachorum* which details the estates belonging to the Archbishop of Canterbury—information of unique importance.

The survey of landownership which was presented to William and his close advisers must have been comforting. Twenty years after Hastings, the whole county was in safe hands. The King himself held four great estates—at Milton Regis, of about 10,000 acres, Faversham, Aylesford, and Dartford. The Church, on whom the Normans relied and who provided them with their civil service, owned half the cultivated land in Kent. The Archbishop owned Sandwich, and 25 manors in various parts of the county, such as Otford, Charing, Wrotham, and Maidstone.

Battle Abbey, founded by William as a penance for Hastings, received the royal Saxon manor of Wye, with rights over much of the Weald, and over Denge-marsh, near Dungeness, including the right to wrecks or to whales stranded on the neighbouring coast. Most of Thanet belonged either to Christ Church or to St Augustine's monasteries, while the Canons of St Martin's at Dover owned about 4,000 acres of land. The rest of the county had by now been parcelled out among six of William's henchmen. Bishop Odo held lands all over Kent, and the scattered nature of his holdings may reflect a considered policy of the Crown to avoid concentration of wealth in the hands of powerful subordinates, though it may equally well be the case that Odo was granted land over many years as the estates of Saxon nobles were seized and the grip of Norman administration tightened. The treachery of Count Eustace of Boulogne seems to have been forgiven, for he has become the lord of the manor of Westerham and of Boughton Aluph. Hugh de Montfort who had fought with the Conqueror at Hastings was an exception to the rule of dispersal. He was made Constable of England and given a block of lands in the south-east of Kent, where he could guard the Channel coast-line.

If the loyalty of the county to William seems assured, the dependence of 99 per cent of Kentishmen upon a superior is even more striking. The total population at the time of Domesday was about 60,000. Of these about 13,000 men are referred to in the Domesday Survey and 11,753 of them are country-dwellers. Eighty-nine per cent of the latter are villeins, borders, or cotters— that is, they held their land on condition that they worked regularly each week on the lord's land, and gave him other feudal dues, which often included military service when necessary— while 10 per cent are serfs or slaves. The livelihood—often, indeed, the very life and happiness—of virtually the whole population was controlled by a tiny collection of lords, either lay or church.

Yet, as time went by, the picture that emerges of life in medieval Kent is not one of universal servility, rather the reverse. We have already seen that before the Conquest the county's peasant was often an independent small holder, working a fair-sized farm, the forerunner of the later 'Yeoman of Kent with his yearly rent'. He was to reappear surprisingly quickly during the middle ages. Villeinage at the time of Domesday in Kent seems to have carried with it less dependence than was the case elsewhere in England,

26　*An artist's impression of Rochester Castle in the later Middle Ages*

and from the beginning, the lord retained less of his land as his own demesne farm and let out more to tenants of various categories. The labour services exacted were less onerous, and vanished more quickly. Only 22 per cent of the county's ploughs, at the time of the survey, were held on the lords' farms; the other 78 per cent were held by the peasants. Thus, there was comparatively little need for tenant labour on the large farms, a fact which, when taken alongside the early reliance on money rents, was to lead to the disappearance of labour services in the county by the fourteenth century. By the end of the next century the county was largely enclosed in self contained farms of differing sizes. The years 1750–1850 which elsewhere in England are known as the years of enclosure saw only the enclosure of some village commons in Kent. So completely had villeinage—the essence of feudalism—vanished by the middle of the medieval period that the proof that a man was born in Kent was sufficient to ensure a man's freedom in any English court. Whatever it may have been in other parts of England, the Peasant's Revolt could not have been a revolt against feudalism in Kent, for by that time the system had ended. The traditional Kentish freedoms, the independence of the Cinque Ports, the traffic along Watling Street from London to the Continent, the cosmopolitan influence of the pilgrims who travelled from all over Europe to the tomb of St Thomas à Becket at Canterbury, the high proportion of forest land (above all in the Weald) which when cleared became the new colonist's possession, all played their part in the early creation of the Kentish yeoman-farmer, whose prosperity and independence of mind became legendary.

The building of castles at key points in the county was carried through efficiently and quickly, and a network of control established which was enough to daunt all but the most determined rebel. Hugh de Montfort controlled his vital territory from his newly-built castle at Saltwood near Hythe which he held as a tenant of the Archbishop. Bishop Gundulf of Rochester rebuilt Rochester Castle, with a classic example of a Norman keep, whose great fist still dominates the Medway today, looking down haughtily on the railway bridge to its right and the M2 road bridge to its left. Further down the Medway, Allington and Tonbridge Castles were built—from Tonbridge an eye could be kept on the Weald—while Eynsford Castle, another manor of the Archbishop's, controlled the Darent valley. The Stour was policed from Canterbury, whose castle, like that at Rochester, was retained in the hands of the King, and from Chilham, whose owner was expected to provide 15 men for the garrison at Dover, where the third of the royal castles was built. If we were to be guided merely by the number of barracks for the occupation forces, no other part of England was so completely under the royal guardsman's boot as Kent.

The garrisoning of Dover Castle during the Middle Ages shows clearly both the nature and the weaknesses of feudalism. In the 1180's Henry II's chief architect at Dover, Master Maurice the Mason, for a fee of one shilling a day, transformed the early Norman fortifications of earthworks, ditches and pallisades into the stone tower keep and inner bailey with walls 20 feet thick which have provided the first sight of England to so many returning travellers from Europe ever since. A garrison of 55 soldiers was needed to man it, and eight Kentish barons were detailed to hold their lands in return for castle-guard service at Dover. The men only served for periods varying from five to eight months a year, and were always changing. They appear frequently to have come from different sub-manors, subservient to one of the main eight *caputs* or head barons, and must have been so diverse in origin as to be militarily most inefficient. Within a generation the service was commuted to an annual money payment, and professional soldiers hired. The newly appointed Constable in 1267, Sir Stephen de Pencestre, set out instructions for the garrison, some of which give sudden vivid insights into the nature of their daily life:

'I At sunset the bridge shall be drawn, and the gates shut; afterwards the guard shall be mounted by 20 warders on the castle walls. . . .

III After the last mount, the sergeants shall turn out of their houses to serve as chief guards. They shall make continual rounds within the Castle to visit the warders on the walls and see that they right loyally keep their watch without going to sleep, by reason that they have the Constable's leave to sleep as much as they like in the daytime.

IV It is established by ancient rule that if a chief guard discover a warder asleep he shall take something from him as he lies, or carry away his staff, or cut a piece out of part of his clothes, to witness against him in case the warder should deny having been asleep, and he shall lose his day's wage, *viz*: 2*d*.

V And if it happen that the sergeant will not make such arrest for pity's sake, or even for life's sake, then he shall be brought before the Constable, and be sentenced to prison *dur et fort*, after which he shall be led to the great gate, in presence of the garrison, and there be expelled the garrison. . . .'

A generation later, we are given details of the garrison's rations. Each man received one half-pound loaf, half a gallon of biscuits, and five pints of wine a day. On 22 days out of 40 he was given fish—five herrings or half a cod. On the other 18 he received half a 'mess' of beef, pork, or mutton. On top of this, he received his ration of cheese and oatmeal and 2*d* a day, one sixth of the chief mason's rate. For these returns, the job could surely never have lacked applicants.

Like most feudal arrangements the duties and privileges of the Cinque Ports arose originally from the weakness of the Crown, from its basic inability to govern and to provide security for its people at home, abroad, or on the high seas. Medieval kings, like their Anglo-Saxon predecessors, found it impossible to provide a professional navy in the manner of Rome, with which the Channel crossing at least could be guarded against public enemies or private piracy. Before the Conquest ship-service was being paid to the King, and Domesday refers specifically to the services of Dover, Sandwich, and Romney. They were to supply 'to the King, once in the year, 20 ships for 15 days, and in each ship were 21 men. This service they did because he had remitted to them the sac and soc.' (That is the right to hold a court and to retain its profits.) Fifteen days seems hardly an adequate period of time from the national point of view, and later its inadequacy was to become glaring. Hythe and Hastings enjoyed a similar position, while Rye and Winchelsea had become full members of the Cinque Ports Confederation, as it was called by the beginning of the fourteenth century.

The ports enjoyed substantial privileges. They were free of all tolls and customs duties, or, to be more precise, of 'lastage, tallage, passage, kayage, rivage, ponsage, and wreck'. They were also 'lovecope-free'—i.e. free to trade unhindered by any monopoly or merchant guild, and had been granted the right to land their fish at Great Yarmouth, dry their nets, and dispose of their catch. The greatest problem the fisherman had, in these days before refrigeration, was to sell his fish before it became bad, and one of the great fish markets was at Great Yarmouth. Here a herring fair was held during the season, and the Cinque Ports were granted the right to appoint bailiffs who controlled the proceedings. Not surprisingly, a bitter feud between the Portsmen and the fishermen of Great Yarmouth arose, which reached a climax in 1297 when the King's fleet, sailing to Sluys, suddenly saw the Cinque Portsmen among its members turn on the neighbouring ships from Yarmouth, destroy 32 of them, and kill over 200 men.

During the height of the Middle Ages Sandwich, which the sea deserted during the sixteenth century, so that it is now a good half hour's walk from the town, was a major port both for international trade and for entry and return to and from the Continent. Before the Conquest the port had belonged to the monastery of Christ Church, and Canute had confirmed possession in his charter of 1023. The monks were given: 'The port of Sandwich and all the revenues of the Haven'—(a finger of land jutted out then from Thanet into the Wantsum Channel, providing a superb sheltered bay, at which ships could lie at anchor)—'on both sides, to whomsoever the ground belongs, from Pepernesse to Mearcesflote, so far as a taper axe can be thrown from a vessel afloat at high water.'

Throughout the Middle Ages and into the sixteenth century,

the town was the scene of dramatic events. In 1164 Becket left England from his own Sandwich, having taken refuge from the King's vengeance in the nearby manor of Eastry, once a royal Saxon palace. Two priests rowed him across Channel in an open boat. On 1 December 1170, he returned. The fishermen of Sandwich and others of the city's poor recognised his flag—the Archbishop's cross—and ran into the water to drag his boat up shore. They knelt on the shingle and begged his blessing. Someone cried 'Blessed is the father of orphans, the judge of widows, blessed is he that cometh in the name of the Lord.' The next day he entered Canterbury in triumphal procession, and by the end of the month he was dead.

A year after signing Magna Carta, John was at the height of his troubles with his barons and with the French. In 1216 the French landed at Pegwell Bay, where John had lined up his mercenaries on the shore but could not rely on them. He stole away by himself, galloping along the Dover road, 'weeping and lamenting'. The French sacked Sandwich, and Louis landed again the next year at the port, burning it on 29 April. But in mid-summer, the French navy was defeated at the battle of Sandwich.

Richard 1 walked from Sandwich, where he had landed on his return from the Crusades and from imprisonment, to Becket's tomb in gratitude for his deliverance and for the successful seige of Acre. During the Hundred Years' War with France Sandwich was a main port of embarkation. The King was frequently at Sandwich, and his household officials infuriated the townsmen by their arrogant behaviour 'perpetrating divers oppressions and grievances, contrary to ancient liberties'. In 1354 all carpenters and shipwrights in the Cinque Ports were arrested and put to work on the King's ships. In 1357 the Black Prince brought back King John of France and his son Philip captive from the battle of Poitiers. Three years later the expedition which departed for France from Sandwich was described by Froissart: 'There never departed out of England before such an army nor so well ordered.' On the Sandwich quays were gathered tents, pavilions, mills, ovens, and forges to 'seethe and to bake and to forge shoes for horses: the carts too, six thousand of them, each drawn by four good horses and many carrying boats of leather, cleverly made to allow three men to row and fish in them, the which did the lords much pleasure in the Lent season.' The King took with him 30 mounted falconers with their hawks, and many greyhounds.

The quays can still be easily imagined by the visitor to Sandwich, stretching along the harbour in between modern Strand Street and the sea, which has long since gone. They were protected in the rear by a stone wall, and in the centre Davies Gate regulated the traffic of Strand Street, which ran along the quays, with Guildhall Street (now the High Street). Not far away stood the Customs' House and the Fisher Gate, close to the Thanet ferry, still there today. Strand Street was the merchant quarter, crowded with storehouses and wine cellars (Sandwich was a major wine importing port) remains of which lie under the road near St Mary's Church, and can still be seen. A porter was paid 3*d* to carry a cask from the haven to a wine cellar, 4*d* if the job entailed loading into a boat.

Men working on the quayside must have marvelled at the exotic goods which they manhandled ashore. Here is a thirteenth century list of customs' dues: 'Wax, figs and raisins, basins by the dozen, almonds and grain by the hundredweight, casks of oil, honey and hogs' lard, dates, mulvell (probably cod), corn, coals, Spanish and Normandy iron, pepper, salmon, wine, salt, tallow, tea, saffron, alum, leather, dressed skins, sugar, whalebone, onions, woolfells, canvas, quicksilver, nuts, lead, and ginger.'[1]

Britain's main export in the Middle Ages was wool, and at the end of the thirteenth century wool exports exceeded 1,000 sacks a year (a sack of wool weighed 364 lbs). In Romney Marsh a steady supply of fine wool lay easily to hand. Parliament had granted the King customs' duty of half a mark (6*s* 8*d*) on every sack of wool exported, a grant which the Crown almost immediately farmed out to Italian bankers, who now proceeded, with other foreign merchants to dominate Sandwich's trade, despite ineffective action from Parliament and bitter protestations from the portsmen themselves. The trade fell away, to revive, for a brief flurry of activity, in the mid-fifteenth century, and reach a peak of 2,520 sacks, exceeding those of London, the leading wool-exporting port. After this the wool trade dwindled, as did the cloth exports which, in 1442–3, had almost equalled those from Southampton, a leading rival. Cloth too was largely in the hands of foreign merchants, and in this year 6,701 cloths were exported by foreigners, including the more recent Hanseatic League representatives, compared to 202 cloths handled by British merchants.

[1] Dorothy Gardiner, *Historic Haven, the Story of Sandwich*, p. 77.

Of all foreign fleets putting into Sandwich the most famous were the Venetian galleys who regularly carried to the outlying northern provinces the riches of the Mediterranean and the East. For the English market sugar and molasses, 'comfits', and preserved fruits were carried, together with 'large coral beads or buttons, Maltese cotton, yarn and spun cotton, silk yarn and saltpetre'.[2] Four galleys, each with 180 oarsmen and 30 archers, sailed from Venice to the Downs, under a careful organisation laid down by the Grand Council of the town. Thence two galleys would sail to London, and two to Sluys, Antwerp or Middleburgh. All four would reassemble at Sandwich for the return journey, and frequently spent frustrating days waiting for their companions to arrive. From 1397 onwards they preferred Rye or Sandwich to the Downs, but like so many others, complained bitterly of the theft of their cargoes by Sandwich men. From 1434 Southampton became the usual port of reassembly. Sandwich was no longer infuriated by their presence or enriched by their trade.

As the Hundred Years' War dragged on, the declining importance of the Cinque Ports became increasingly obvious. The Crown grew dissatisfied with their ships of 30 to 60 tons, manned by crews of 21 men. They demanded ships of 100 tons and more, manned by 65 men. The Portsmen provided a mere fraction of the total fleet, compared with Yarmouth, Southampton, Portsmouth, Poole or other ports. A series of French raids—often in answer to raids by Portsmen on northern French ports—caused serious damage. Rye and Winchelsea were badly hurt, and at Hythe, the burgesses, through raids, fire and pestilence were talking of abandoning the town, if Henry IV had not remitted their service for a while. In August 1457 an expedition set sail from Honfleur for Sandwich with 60 ships, 4,000 men, and artillery. They disembarked early on a Sunday morning and forced their entry into the town. The French killed the Mayor, Bailiff and other officials, abducted some wealthy townsmen and their wives, and pillaged the town. The Mayor's official dress still contains a black robe of mourning for the disaster.

The indiscipline of the Portsmen hastened their end. The men of the Cinque Ports were everybody's enemies, not only those of the northern French fishermen. They had a standing feud with the men of Fowey and other west-country ports. In 1242 they were given the royal authority to plunder the French coast, so long as

<hr>

[2] *ibid.*, p. 130.

they spared the churches, and gave the King one fifth of the loot. In fact the Portsmen killed and pillaged English merchants and their cargoes as well as French. In 1314 Winchelsea equipped two ships to protect the coast against pirates, one of which committed at least six piratical acts within a month. Merchants from southern Europe offered a tempting prey. A galley from Majorca was seized by the men of Sandwich, full of 'divers cloths', silver, copper, and tin, to the value of £610. The cargo was shared out in the port and the captain and crew, having been robbed even of their clothes, were kindly 'permitted so to depart'. The men of the Cinque Ports were a wild and unreliable band, and the House of Commons seems to have been fully justified when it complained that they provided little enough service in return for their privileges. Finally nature settled their fate, when the coast line changed, and the sea receded. At Romney, Rye, Winchelsea, Hythe, and Sandwich, the ports were left stranded by the end of the sixteenth century, and Dover only avoided a similar fate by royal support and their own determined efforts.

In the Middle Ages, as in previous periods, Canterbury was the county's largest and most influential settlement, the only Kentish borough which possessed a national and international standing. In Henry II's reign it was paying, in the list of aids and tallages compiled by the Crown, 100 marks a year, a figure which was exceeded only by London (1,000 marks), Northampton (300), York (200), and Dunwich, Winchester and Lincoln (150 each).* In 1170 Archbishop Thomas à Becket was murdered in his own cathedral by four knights acting on Henry's orders and pilgrimages, which developed the wealth and reputation of the city, began to his tomb which soon became one of the wonders of Europe. Though the existence of its two great monasteries, and the presence of the English Church's senior archbishop, a clerical concentration which was powerful enough even before the pilgrimages, made Canterbury unusual—it has been reckoned that about one in 10 of the population worked for the Church—the picture of medieval town-life received from the monastic records is of more than local interest, so comprehensive is its detail. Two generalisations about medieval towns which are frequently made are contradicted straightaway. There were no common fields belonging to the town in which the townsmen owned strips of land by right, and the citizens' houses sprawled at their ease well

* I owe these figures, as I owe the whole of this passage on medieval Canterbury, to Dr William Urry's *Canterbury under the Angevin Kings*, and would like here to pay tribute to that remarkable book, the result of a lifetime's knowledge.

outside the city's walls. The men of Canterbury were townsmen, not farmers living within the city walls for protection who commuted from the town to the surrounding countryside each working day. There seems to have been not one man within the late twelfth century city who was dependent for his livelihood mainly upon agriculture (though of course, many homes grew food or kept animals—driven out of the gates early in the morning and recalled before the curfew bell each night—as a sideline). As for the general belief that homes were universally huddled within the walls for fear of attack from foreign raiders or anarchic lords, Canterbury's records do not bear it out. A long growth of ribbon development stretched out to Barton on the Sturry Road, half a mile from the city's Northgate, while fair-sized settlements were also to be found outside Westgate, on the London road, in the area of Wincheap, and outside Burgate and Newingate.

Within the walls there was a fair amount of space, and the people, if they lived in a house at all, were not particularly cramped. Children who survived death in childbirth or infancy were not numerous, so families were small, and Dr William Urry has written: 'It does seem that scores of modern shops do business today in half the space occupied by a twelfth-century citizen.' Most houses were wooden-framed, with wattle-and-daub laid between the beams, though there were at least 30 stone houses. They were flush with the street, and thatched, which produced the frequent and terrible fires which were part of each generation's experience. There were about 200 shops serving the 3,000–4,000 population at any one time. They were tiny, seven-foot wide or narrower, and may well have been more like stalls, with nobody living above or behind them. Markets were held in and without the city—for cattle, slaughtered meat, fish, waggons (unless, as some argue, Wincheap was the site of a wine market, rather than a wain market) timber, and salt. There were 15 cooks, some of whom probably also worked as monastic servants, serving the public from cook-shops, bakers, alewives, fodder merchants, cornmongers, and vintners (until 1200 the monks had a vineyard on the slopes outside the northern city walls). References to butchers are rare, though there were two flesh-shambles, so slaughtermen must have existed.

By the thirteenth century the mint at Canterbury, where the first English penny was struck—in Offa's reign—was the only

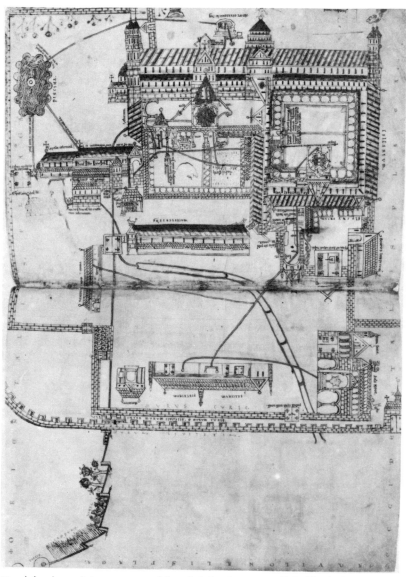

27 *A drawing made in 1130–1174 of the cathedral and monastery, Christ Church, Canterbury*

legal mint outside London, and several moneyers were at work in the city. Goldsmiths, of whom there were 12 in the early thirteenth-century town, also leant money, as did the Jewish community, who lived in the central business area around the King's Bridge, and Stour Street, where the synagogue stood (modern Jewry Lane bears witness to the past). They enjoyed friendly relationships with the townsmen and with Christ Church, who borrowed freely from them. The building trade is quite well represented in the list of the city's occupations, with seven masons, eight carpenters, a glazier, a plumber, two thatchers, and a painter. There are some physicians, a tailor, and various weavers. The leather trade must have been booming. Tanners are listed, along with three glovers, and three saddlers. Footwear was produced by four corvisers, four cordwainers, and one sutor, and the ampoller's bottles were probably made of leather. He would have sold well to pilgrims, who liked to carry away with them the water of St Thomas. The Stour was thick with mills, in and outside the walls.

The Church was a major employer of a wide variety of men, ranging from the arrogant ecclesiastics who all too often formed part of the Archbishop's entourage, along with quick-witted and hard-working young aspirants to high office in Church and State (Becket himself had once been one) to priests serving the small private chapels of rich men, or clergy serving one of the city's 22 parish churches. There were 80 priests and clerks in the city in the late-twelfth century, several of whom were sons of priests, for clerical marriage was still allowed, though Becket himself is known to have been strongly opposed to it. The servants of the monks at Christ Church were as numerous as their masters. There were about 100 of each, and the monastery too was surrounded by a large number of poor, such as odd-job men (like the man who cleaned out the cathedral drains each week) men who stood around hoping to be hired, if only for the day, and plain beggars. Then there were the hawkers, always on the move and often on the run, the fuel-vendors, the washerwomen, and, at the very bottom of the medieval pack of cards, the 'unthanks' or squatters, who stole in and out of the shadows of the great city.

Though the cathedral building must have stood out high above the thatched beehive-like houses in a manner which could not have failed to impress and overawe, the approach to it was squalid.

Visitors came to it through a narrow alley, past crowded houses, where the fire had started which burnt down the first Norman Cathedral, a well, and a forge, round a bend and along the wall face, and so into the graveyard. The bells from the Cathedral towers dominated the life of the streets and drowned the citizens' conversation. The castle which, as we have seen, was kept in the King's own hands, formed part of the walls, which followed the Roman circuit throughout their length. They enclosed the whole city, with towers added in the fourteenth century, placed at regular intervals along their course, and numerous gates into the city, which were closed at nightfall. Three of the gates were surmounted by churches. Outside the gates were placed the bars as an extra defence, the one in the Sturry road being half-a-mile from the North Gate at Coldharbour Lane. At road junctions stood the crosses—St Dunstan's Cross, outside the Westgate, marked the London road, for instance, while the vital wells were to be found both within and without the city.

The system of savage punishment which typified the time was obvious to every citizen. In the High Street stood the pillory, to the south of it the gaol, while the Prior of Christ Church had his gallows outside the town. There is reason to believe that the ordeal pit, where the medieval system of justice appealed to the arbitration of fate by means of the ordeal by fire, water, or battle, also lay outside the city walls.

The Church permeated medieval life to its very roots, and its presence could be seen everywhere. Shrines were to be found at the roadside, or in clearings among the thousands of acres of forest, and the traveller would genuflect as he passed them, or the housewife kneel before them with her sick child or her daily burden of anxiety. Every baby born in a village would be brought for christening by the priest in the parish church, and everybody was buried after his short life in the village churchyard. Attendance at Mass on Sundays would be almost universal, and on Monday morning the priest would bring the body of Christ to the sick or old who had yesterday stayed abed. Woefully ignorant though he most frequently was, the priest was the nearest thing to an educated man to be found in a Kentish village and it is impossible to exaggerate his influence as Sunday after Sunday, on work days and at festivals, he spoke to the people of the teachings of Christ and the mysteries of life and death. Though the murals,

28   *The South Doorway of Barfreston Church, near Dover*

the statues of the saints, the stations of the cross and the vivid wall hangings have gone, it is possible still to recapture the villagers' world, which the boroughs, with their tiny populations and intimate divisions into parishes, reflected, by a visit to one of the many hundreds of parish churches in the county. The Norman Church at Barfreston, near Dover, the Early English churches at Ash, near Sandwich, or at Faversham, and the fifteenth century Perpendicular churches at Cranbrook or Biddenden in the Weald are just a few out of many examples, while the Romney Marsh churches are a unique little confederation. One characteristic shared by many of the county's parish churches is their lightness, as if they are built in the heavens themselves, a quality which derives from their comparative lack of stained glass.

All over Kent there were other signs of the Church's presence in the form of monasteries, nunneries, hospitals and, when these ways of life had lost their earlier idealism, friaries. The Conquest had introduced a new period of monastic foundations and reformations, led by the energetic Norman archbishop Lanfranc— who was Italian by birth, though he came to England via the monastery of St Stephen at Caen—and by 1300 there were nearly 30 religious houses in the county. Though they varied considerably in size and in wealth—none could match the two great Canterbury foundations with their vast estates—and though new orders were founded after the Conquest, they all had in common the belief that a life of disciplined prayer, of service to the poor, and of scholarship, could redeem the violence and false values of the world around them. If they have been accused of isolation from the life of the surrounding community, the fact that many of the monks were themselves, as Dr Urry has shown with regard to Christ Church, local men, must have decreased animosities.

No justification, however, can be found for the wealth of the great monasteries, and for the vast quantity of food which Geraldus of Wales saw served at their tables on a visit to Christ Church. Sixteen courses were served one Trinity Sunday, he tells us, while the Prior loved to send delicacies from his high table down to privileged individuals who were eating in the body of the hall below him. St Benedict had forbidden the eating of meat, but his followers evaded his order by avoiding the eating of meat in the refectory (or dining hall) as they were instructed, but eating lavishly of beef, mutton, and pork in other parts of the monastery.

29 *An eighteenth-century print of St John's Hospital, Canterbury*

They did themselves proud on fish—one monk's dish, it was laid down, should consist of two soles or one plaice, four herrings or eight mackerel—while the best French wine was imported through Sandwich for their benefit.

More to their credit was the work of the 40 'hospitals' which were often attached to monastic foundations. Here specifically the work of helping the poor, the old, the sick, or travellers was carried on, in small institutions devoted to their care. Lanfranc founded St Nicholas at Harbledown for lepers and laid down that the lepers should be cared for by a chaplain and 'skilful, patient, and kindly watchers'. The historian of the hospital has described the patients' appearance as follows: '. . . In medieval times the leper brothers had a russet gown and scapular each and the sisters a mantle, with oxhide boots fastened with leather and extending beyond the middle of the shin, the men wearing hoods also and the women thick double veils, white within and black without, presumably to cover the ravages of the disease.'[3]

At the same time Lanfranc founded a hospital in Northgate, Canterbury, for a 100 old and needy men and women with 'watchers' to care for them in sickness, and a religious community across the road to look after their spiritual needs. St John's Hospital still continues its work, with almshouses brought up to date, and a resident nurse and lay warden, a quiet reminder that the Church, though it has continually deserted its ideals, has always returned to them.

The friars, and especially the Franciscans or greyfriars, were totally wedded by their foundations to a life of personal poverty

[3] D. Ingram Hill, *The Ancient Hospitals and Almshouses of Canterbury*. Pub. Canterbury Public Library, 1969.

and service to the poor. Even before St Francis's death in 1226, nine of his followers had landed at Dover, and a strange sight they must have formed, dressed in 'coarse russet garments, patched with old sacking, and girded around their loins with a piece of old rope, the ends knotted to keep it from fraying.'[4] When they reached Canterbury, they were entertained for a couple of days by the monks of Christ Church. Four of them set off for London, but five remained, and were given a plot of ground on a small island in the Stour, a swampy, mist-bound unsettled part of the city, by the Master of the Poor Priest's Hospital, whose garden it was. Here they built their first friary. This was probably constructed in accordance with their founder's teaching that poor building was as important as poor living, and consisted of wattle cells, the walls filled in with dried grass or mud, and a small chapel, an unconsecrated building which could sensibly be put to any secular use, with mass celebrated at a portable altar. Later they moved—something over 30 of them—into more permanent and comfortable buildings nearby, the gift of various well-to-do citizens, for from the first the friars seem to have attracted help from a number of wealthy men, help whose effect on the quality of their life over the years may well have not been entirely beneficial. Here they pursued a life of aid to the poor and sick, of assistance to the local parish priests, of teaching and of scholarship, until they were finally suppressed by Henry VIII.

Many of the hospitals existed to give shelter to travellers, along the lines of the Hospital for Poor Pilgrims built on the bridge over the Stour in the middle of Canterbury High Street. This was 'for the maintenance of poor pilgrims and other infirm persons resorting thither to remain until they are healed of their infirmities, for the poor, for persons going to Rome, for others coming to Canterbury and needing shelter, and for lying-in women.' They slept on rushes on the floor, washed in the river, and perhaps received some food. It was the pilgrims, above all, who created such an untypical number of travellers in medieval Kent, and they seem to have begun streaming along the road from London or into the Channel ports shortly after the murder of Archbishop Thomas à Becket. In the one year of 1420—the second centenary of the erection of the saint's shrine—they were said to number 100,000.

For 250 years they came from all over Europe and from as far

4 C. C. Cotton, *The Grey Friars of Canterbury*, p. 2.

The forme and figure of the Shrine of Tho: Becket of Canterbury

Siluer gilt 60 vnces

Siluer gilt 60 vnces

Tem: H 8.

As aboue the stone worke was first of wood Tem as of gold set 7... stone wrought vpon with gold men then agayn with Jewels of gold at fron 10, or 12 together stamped with gold into the ground of gold the chief such as 6. or 8. men could not conuuy or out of the church an Angell of gold poynting ther rub offred ther by a king of france into a ring and wear it on his thomb

this chest of Iron con bones of Thomas Beck[et] fell with at mi... the pope

30   Becket's Shrine, from a burnt Manuscript of Henry VIII's time

north as Iceland to give thanks, or to seek help, to be healed, or to gawp, to travel for the sake of it or for the pleasure of the company. Their easy pace as they rode along gave rise to the verb 'to canter'. Becket's death was said to have been followed within two days by the first miracle, when the blind wife of a Sussex knight, who had made a vow to 'Saint Thomas, martyr precious to Christ', was cured. Miracles followed by the hundred. Blood, scraped by monks and townsmen from the floor where Becket's body lay, was claimed to have healed the deaf, the lame, and the blind, and to have cured cases of leprosy, epilepsy, and dropsy. Within three years Becket had been canonised, and the pilgrims poured into the city, seeking the ampullas or bottles of his blood heavily diluted with water. On the fiftieth anniversary of his death Archbishop Stephen Langton ordered the translation of the martyr's body from the crypt of the cathedral, where the monks had hastily buried it, to a place behind the high altar. Here a coffer, covered with gold and encrusted with jewels, had been made for the body. One hundred years later the saint's skull was enclosed in a reliquary formed in the shape of a human head made of gold and precious stones. Edward I gave gold brooches for the shrine's adornment and other jewellery and in 1299 offered the captured royal crown of Scotland. Most splendid of all was the great jewel—the Régale of France—which Louis VII of France had given. Shortly before its destruction Erasmus had visited the shrine and reported: 'Every part glistened and shone and sparkled with rare and very large jewels, some of them bigger than a goose's egg.'

This was the climax of the pilgrims' journey, as they went on their knees up the stone steps, which are deeply worn today by their imprint, and came from the shadows into the holiest of all the holy places, vividly lit by the scores of wax tapers which burnt around the shrine. Long before Henry VIII had smashed the shrine, scattering the saint's remains so that nobody knows where, if anywhere, they lie today and carted off the gold and jewels to London in a long procession of wagons, the cult of St Thomas had died away, so that even the third centenary of the saint's translation in 1520 was uncelebrated. In 1532 the offerings at the shrine totalled £13, as compared to an average of £545 a year in the 1370s, the period of Chaucer's *Canterbury Tales*, and the height of the shrine's attraction.

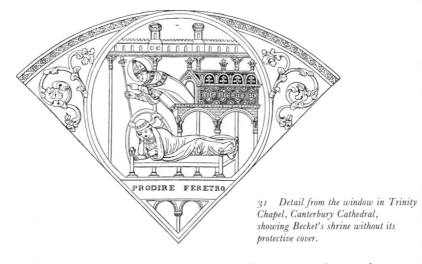

PRODIRE FERETRO

31 *Detail from the window in Trinity Chapel, Canterbury Cathedral, showing Becket's shrine without its protective cover.*

Yet as always the great majority of the county's people, men, women, and children from the time that they could walk worked on the land. And, again as always, we can only guess at their daily life, for they have left no record behind them, since they could not read or write. Work occupied most of their lives, for they could neither retire in old age, nor afford candles for the evenings when they returned from the fields. The numerous saints' days provided some welcome breaks in the grinding routine, but in general it is probably true to say that when they were not working they were sleeping, and when they could no longer perform a full day's work they died. In Kent, as we have seen, the burdens of villeinage were comparatively light, and small farmers gained their independence early. Great numbers of people worked on the church estates, and once again we are indebted to the methodical records kept by Christ Church Priory for the picture of the big estate's manner of work which emerges from them.

By the end of the eleventh century Christ Church possessed estates which were scattered over eight southern counties and included land in Ireland. The priory owned 21 estates in Kent, covering most of the county, though the Weald was only occupied at its fringes. The estates were looked at as a whole, and different land specialised in different corn crops, more oats, for instance, being grown in west Kent, the Weald, and Romney Marsh, and more barley in east Kent, particularly Thanet. Production

84

was for the market, particularly London, and for export through Sandwich. The work was carried out by agricultural labourers who lived on the estates. At Monkton in Thanet for instance, the permanent staff in 1307 included 17 plough men, and a harrower, four shepherds and a lambherd, a swineherd, two cowherds, and a cheesemaker. They were paid three shillings a year plus food, whereas the sergeant (or bailiff) received £2 14s 10d, the hayward £1 14s 1d and the beadle 13s 4d.

The monks of Christ Church were some of the most advanced farmers in the country. They were careful savers and users of manure from farmyards, sheepfolds, and dove's droppings, and spread marl on their newly embanked lands in Romney Marsh. Large-scale sheep-farming had been pioneered in England by the monks, especially the Cistercians. Christ Church concentrated its flocks on Thanet and the Romney marshes, and sold their wool to Italian merchants who, as we have seen, were based in Sandwich. Sheep were valuable not only for wool, but for mutton, ewes' milk, and ewes' cheese, while their manure was always useful. The peak of the estates' sheep farming successes—like that of other branches of their agricultural production—came about the year 1320. After that there was a sharp decline caused, it would seem, by successive plagues, drought, and sea flooding—as well as by taxation and the monopoly held by the Merchant Staplers over the wool trade. Nearly a third of monastic flocks were killed during the terrible years of 1324–6. Some of the best Thanet sheep-runs were empty, though the Romney Marsh run was always maintained and even increased.

The monastic estates were particularly remarkable for the ways in which marshland was drained and the seawalls embanked. This work was to be found at Seasalter and at Cliffe, in northern Kent, and at Lyden, near Sandwich, and Monkton in the east of the county. But above all, it was to be found in the Romney Marsh, half of which the Archbishop and the Prior owned, where the encroachment of the sea reached its climax in the fierce storms of 1287–8, completely changing the course of the river Rother, so that it flowed out at Rye instead of Romney Haven, and flooded a huge stretch of land between Appledore and Winchelsea.

By the middle of the medieval period the Weald had been mainly colonised and, like the Marsh, enclosed in self-contained farms. The method of piecemeal settlement produced hamlets, and scattered farmsteads rather in the manner which we have previously seen as typical of pre-Conquest Kent in general, whereas by this time east Kent had developed many of the nucleated villages, concentrated around the church, the green, and the public house that we think of as the typical English village. The Weald had known industrial activity from the earliest time in its iron industry, and with its timber used first in house and later in ship construction. By the end of the medieval period the new and most profitable industry of cloth-making had grown up in Cranbrook.

The little town's prosperity started with a deliberate decision by Edward III to establish a cloth industry in England which could compete with the Netherlands' monopoly. He granted passports to clothmakers and their servants from Ghent to enter England for the purpose of 'working wool and exercising their mystery'. From 1331 onwards they settled in the country, and the new industry took root in Cranbrook and in the surrounding Wealden villages. Running water necessary for the fulling mills was to be found in the many small streams around the town, which were easy to dam; marl or fuller's earth was on the spot, as was an endless quantity of oak for building mills. Cloth of good quality could be bought from local weavers, who wove the fleeces from Thanet or the nearby Marsh. Soon the cloth was being pressed and scoured under the heavy wooden hammers of the fulling mills, which rose and fell with the turning of the water wheel. Later it was stretched on racks in nearby fields, held together by iron hooks known as 'tenter hooks'.

The clothier first of all bought the wool and distributed it to the cottages in the local villages for carding and spinning. The spun wool was then passed from spinner to weaver, fuller to dyer, until finally it was ready to be carried to London or to Sandwich, if it was to be exported. The industry called for the type of merchant-employer who was many years later to provide the capital for the industrial revolution. Once again, Kent was in advance of the rest of the country, though the Wealden cloth industry declined gradually into insignificance after it had reached its peak in the reigns of Elizabeth and James I.

Beneath the surface of medieval society, violent currents of grievance were always to be found, and the period after the Black Death, in which anything up to one third of the English

86

people lost their lives, was one of social upheaval culminating in the Peasants' Revolt of 1381. Accounts of the Black Death are to be found in the writings of two monks, Stephen Birchington of Canterbury and William Dene of Rochester. Birchington refers to 'such a scarcity and dearth of priests that the parish churches remained almost unserved, and beneficed persons, for fear of death, left the care of their benefices'. William Dene paints a grimmer picture for the west of the county: 'The mortality was so great that none could be found to carry the corpses to the grave. Men and women bore their own offspring on their shoulders to the church, and cast them into a common pit. From these there came so great a stench that hardly anyone dared to cross the cemetery.'

Attempts to reimpose labour services on villeins after the Black Death, often regarded as a major cause of the Peasants' Revolt, could have had little effect in Kent, where feudalism was a thing of the past. But high rents may well have been a grievance, and there were probably various surviving exactions and restrictions on tenant farmers or on labourers which were fiercely resented, as the rebels seem to have been keen to destroy all records or rolls which they found in the houses of the wealthy when they broke into them. There were always bitter feelings in Canterbury against the ruling oligarchy to be played upon, while the resentment of countrymen against their landlords, particularly if they were churchmen, could easily be aroused. The interminable wars with France affected Kent more than elsewhere. Taxes were levied and men recruited for the wars, while the indignation felt at the government's weakness, which could allow the French to burn Gravesend in 1380, and abduct many of its leading citizens, was intense. At the height of the revolt the next year, the rebels posted special guards on the south coast from among their members, while the main body made for London. The teachings of the Lollards and of rebel priests like John Ball must have led men to question the social order and the moral basis of existing society, while the poll tax acted as the final occasion for the revolt which started over the Thames in Essex when a crowd killed some members of a tax commissioner's party. On 4 June Robert Cave, a baker, led an angry crowd into Dartford. Two days later several thousands of men massed around Rochester Castle and forced its capitulation.

From now on events moved swiftly; from Rochester the rebels marched along the Medway to Maidstone, where they chose Wat Tyler as their leader and released the priest John Ball from imprisonment in the Archbishop's gaol. We know nothing of Tyler's antecedents—he is said by some to have come from Essex rather than Kent—but John Ball was already known as a rebel priest. This was his third imprisonment in ecclesiastical gaols. He had been excommunicated earlier, and he had long urged the people in Colchester and elsewhere to withhold tithes from unworthy clergy and to work for the social equality which Christ desired. He was carried now by a triumphant crowd, who sacked the houses of royal officials, lawyers, and unpopular landlords as they went along to Canterbury which Tyler seized on 10 June. The Archbishop was in London, but the rebels pillaged his palace, and Tyler executed three men whom the people of Canterbury handed over to him as 'traitors'. He must have felt the need to maintain momentum for the rebels left Canterbury the next day and on the evening of 12 June camped on Blackheath.

It was here that John Ball preached his sermon on the text:

> *When Adam dalf and Eve span*
> *Who was then a gentleman?*

a couplet which was already going the rounds. It must count as the first coherent statement of the belief in equality of which we have record in England.

The rest belongs to the history of England rather than that of Kent. For a time the rebels had London at their mercy. Houses were fired, 200 immigrants mostly Flemings and Lombards lynched, Sudbury the Archbishop of Canterbury and the Treasurer, Sir Robert Hales, executed by the rebels. But Tyler was killed in a scuffle around the 14 year old King Richard, who acted with remarkable coolness to save both his life and his authority. The pendulum swung. Sober men were appalled by the picture of a great city lying at the mercy of a crowd which had grown completely out of hand. The King promised an end to serfdom, the abolition of all feudal services, and even later appeared prepared to concede the confiscation of the church estates and agree that 'no legal status should differentiate one man from another, save the king alone'. But he neither kept nor intended to keep his promises. When the crowds began to make for home, exhausted and psychologically past their peak, the authorities struck. Order was reimposed, with remarkable speed. Wat Tyler's lieutenant, Jack Straw, was executed, and though John Ball fled, he was captured and, in front of the young King's eyes, hung, drawn and quartered at St Albans. There remained only the special assize to deal with those who had led the revolt in Kent and Essex. In the circumstances it is surprising that only 110 men were executed in the two counties, though more were probably killed without trial. The official records show how serious the revolt was in Kent, and how widely it spread, though the villages involved are largely east of the Medway.

Kent was involved in another serious revolt in the fifteenth century, when wars with France and fights between rival groups of nobles sporadically affected the county. This time the aims of the rebels seem to have been mainly political, concerned with the incompetence of a government which had lost much of France and could not even defend its own coasts.

The rebellion came mainly from west Kent and the Weald— men from Smarden and Pluckley were named in hundreds—and was supported by a large number of gentry who summoned the rebels as if they were acting by lawful authority. (There was a Twysden among them, and three Culpeppers, famous Kentish names.) It started at Ashford, and in June 1450 20,000 men camped on Blackheath, led by Jack Cade. The leaders submitted to the King their 'Articles of Complaint', which attacked the traitors who had lost France, and wasted the king's treasures. Henry vi ordered the rebels to disperse, and they retreated towards Sevenoaks followed by the King's troops. At Bromley Cade's men ambushed some of the force, whereupon many members of it mutinied and joined the rebels. Cade now returned to the capital which he entered in strength on 3 July after the King had left it. He beheaded the hated Lord Say, lord of Knole, near Sevenoaks, together with William Cromer, his son-in-law, Sheriff of Kent. Say was particularly unpopular in the Knole area, while Cromer was regarded as an extortionate tax-collector. But once again the rebels grew out of hand, though Cade and the leaders had at first acquired a reputation for disciplining their men, and London swung against them. Most of the rebels dispersed when offered a royal pardon. Cade, tricked by the King, was hunted into Sussex and killed. His body was beheaded and quartered, the head being exhibited on London Bridge. His Kentish supporters were harried during the rest of the year, and the King himself led a commission to try offenders. Twenty-nine died as the result of it, eight in Canterbury, when the King was there, at Candlemas (2 February) 1451. The people called it the 'harvyste of hedys'. When Henry returned to London he found the heads of nine more men of Kent—this time from Rochester—to greet him on London Bridge.

5
Kent during the Reformation

The Church in Kent had long occupied an apparently dominating position. Its presence was everywhere to be seen. In the towns, as in the villages, the parish church was the place of regular worship for virtually the entire population. In Canterbury, the shrine of Saint Thomas à Becket had quickly become the town's major industry. Monasteries and nunneries were to be found in considerable numbers throughout the county, apart from the Weald and the Romney Marsh.

Half the county's cultivated land belonged to the Church, a staggering proportion. It must have seemed as if the Roman Catholic Church's position, not only in the power structure, but in the intimate places of the people's daily life, was permanently assured. Yet within a few years during the 1530s, the religious houses, hospitals, and orders had gone, leaving hardly a trace behind them, while the connection with the pope, which had lasted for nearly 1,000 years, was abruptly and finally ended. The extraordinary rapidity of events showed clearly enough the superficial nature of the Roman Catholic Church's apparently impregnable position.

Well before Thomas Cromwell sent out his commissioners to inspect the county's religious houses, inspections which, as all the world knew, would be rapidly followed by their dissolution, the vitality of their life had reached a low point. St Augustine's Abbey was inhabited by 30 monks in the 1520s; at its height it had been the home of five times that number. Several small houses were closed altogether by the Church authorities, such as the nunnery at Higham, where the sole inhabitants, three nuns, were dismissed for living unworthy lives and the convent given by Bishop Fisher to St John's College, Cambridge. The abbeys at Lesnes and Tonbridge were also closed in 1525, and their wealth was granted to Wolsey's new college, Christ Church at Oxford. When Archbishop Warham visited Dover, he found only 12 monks at Dover Priory while the hospital of St Mary or Maison Dieu, in the same town, was served by a master and five brethren.

Most Church land had been let to tenants for many years, so the dissolution of the monasteries had little effect in the countryside. The monks of Christ Church, for instance, had long since withdrawn from their previous work of reclamation on the Romney Marshes. With their tenants' rents they built the nave of their Cathedral, and constructed the central Bell Harry Tower, with its four slender pinnacles, magnificent examples of the Perpendicular style, still forming the first inland landmark that strikes the Continental visitor who lands at Dover, and takes the London road.

There can be little doubt that the 'religious'—monks, nuns and friars—had achieved a bad name long before the King's dispute about his marriage, and his insistent demands for money produced the official attack that ended their way of life. The parish clergy had little time for them, either through an honest belief in their own superior abilities, so far as parish work went, or jealousy. Archbishop Warham, the last Roman Catholic archbishop, conducted a visitation of his diocese in 1511, when he was clearly concerned by reports both of corruption and laxity among his clergy, and rumours that heretical teaching was circulating. His visitors reported a common cause of grievance, absenteeism among the monks who were supposed to serve a parish, and whose rare appearances compared poorly with the attentions of previous parish priests. At Westgate, for instance, where the Church of the Holy Cross was meant to be served by St Gregory's at Canterbury: 'there is no secular priest that serveth the cure these three years, but the prior of St Gregory's of Canterbury causeth one of his own canons to serve it, the which goeth to the priory every night and when we should have him, oftentimes in the night season, we cannot have him'.[1]

If a determined king, assisted by a competent and single-minded minister, decided to close down the monasteries, and confiscate their wealth—and such a policy had frequently been threatened in the past—he would find his opponent isolated,

[1] *The Victoria County History of Kent*, Vol II, Ecclesiastical History p. 65.

almost friendless, with his confidence badly sapped from within. Such a king was Henry VIII and such a minister was Thomas Cromwell. The first signs of trouble between Church and State were to be found in the case of Elizabeth Barton, who became known as the Nun or Holy Maid of Kent.

Elizabeth Barton, who was born in 1509 was a domestic servant in the household of Thomas Cobb, steward of the Archbishop of Canterbury's estates at Aldington, near Lympne, on the lower slopes of the Downs overlooking Romney Marsh. Her story reveals an attitude of mind, both among the educated and uneducated, which is still completely medieval. One has only to imagine the year of her birth as being 40 years later, with the report of her experiences circulating not in the 1520s but in the 1560s, to realise how swiftly and how completely the English Reformation triumphed. Had she been born in 1559 we would never have heard of her.

When Elizabeth was 16 she seems to have suffered a number of epileptic seizures, and to have lain in a trance for days on end. During this time she appeared to possess prophetic gifts, for she 'told wondrously things done in other places, whilst she was neither herself present not yet heard no report thereof'. Sometimes her cries were 'of marvellous holiness in rebuke of sin and vice', or concerned 'the seven deadly sins and the ten commandments'. She maintained that the Blessed Virgin had appeared to her and foretold her cure in the well-known Chapel of Our Lady at the village of Court-the-Street nearby. Cobb was impressed with her sincerity and power and sent for the parish priest. He watched her, believed her possessed by the Holy Ghost and passed on his findings to the Archbishop. Warham sent a message to the girl, that she was not 'to hide the goodness and the works of God'. Elizabeth was taken to the Chapel on the Feast of the Assumption (15 August 1525) and cured before the image of the Holy Virgin in the presence of 2,000 people. The Chapel became a place of pilgrimage, and in the autumn the Archbishop ordered Elizabeth to enter the convent of St Sepulchre near Canterbury, where Edward Bocking, a monk from Christ Church, became her confessor and director.

Warham was most impressed with her character and powers and introduced her to Wolsey, whom she rebuked for neglecting his responsibilities. The King attached little importance to her

32 *John Fisher, Bishop of Rochester, by Holbein*

prophecies but asked Sir Thomas More to examine her. He too thought her prophecies 'such as any simple woman might speak of her own wit', but regarded her with utmost seriousness, writing to her humbly as if she was spiritually far more advanced than he was. Bishop Fisher too had an interview with her and was reported to have wept with joy at her revelations. The fact was later to be used against him at his trial.

Unfortunately, Elizabeth did not confine her pronouncements to matters of private spiritual difficulty or insight. From an early stage, from the moment she heard of the rumours that were circulating the Court about Henry's determination to divorce

Queen Catherine and marry Anne Boleyn, now installed at Hever Castle, she opposed the suggestion with extraordinary frankness. Pope Clement was threatened with disaster if he encouraged the King. Henry sent for her, and was told plainly of the wrath that would devour him if he forsook Queen Catherine. He would no longer be 'king of this realm and would die a villain's death'. She tried to see Henry again later when, shortly before his marriage to Anne, he passed through Canterbury and she burst in upon him, trying to terrify him into a change of heart. Whatever may be thought of her wisdom, nobody could deny Elizabeth's courage. By now her fate was assured. After his marriage in 1533 Henry and Cromwell, assisted by the new Archbishop Cranmer, were determined to establish their new national Church. Their opponents were few enough, but Elizabeth Barton was certainly at the centre of what Catholic party there was. Cranmer made the first move, interrogating her gently at his Otford Palace, but in September the Attorney General, Sir Christopher Hales, a Canterbury man, was ready to strike. 'As I can catch them, one after another,' he wrote to Cromwell from Canterbury, 'I will send them to you.' Bocking, the parish priest from Aldington who first had drawn his superiors' attentions to the maid's powers, the author of the pamphlet that described the miracles at Court-the-Street, Hugh Rich, late warden of the Greyfriars, Canterbury, Richard Risby, present warden, and Elizabeth herself were all committed to the Tower. She was brought before a great gathering of judges, nobles, and members of the Council who debated for three days 'the crimes, or rather the foolish superstitions of the Nun and her adherents'. At the conclusion of the Chancellor's speech the gathering cried out—'To the stake with her!' but the authorities had not finished with her yet. She now declared that her revelations had been imaginary, a 'confession' which she was said to have repeated on the scaffold. The pressures upon her during the months between her first interview with Cranmer in July 1533 and her execution of April 1534 can be all too readily imagined. With her died Bocking, the friars, and the Aldington parish priest, in the usual revolting circumstances. Elizabeth died a traitor, so her goods became the property of the Crown—'an old matteres seven corsse schettes. . . . A lyttell old dyaper towell. . . . An old mantell and a kyrtell.'

Next year, in 1535, Thomas Cromwell began his campaign to

dissolve the monasteries, and within five years his object had been achieved. The Prior and monks of Christ Church had tried to forestall trouble by signing the necessary acknowledgement of royal supremacy early in December 1534. They had been terrified by the complicity of Bocking and others of their number with the 'Nun' and had fulsomely disassociated themselves from any suggestion of favour towards her. This had little effect on Cromwell, who was openly boasting that he would make his master the richest prince in Christendom. In order to do so he was bound to move promptly against Christ Church and St Augustine's and to grasp the great wealth that had been grafted over the years onto Becket's tomb. In October 1535 the visitation of commissioner Richard Layton, a famous harrier of monks, began. He was critical of the monks' manner of life, as was to be expected, and issued injunctions which included the prohibition of secular shops within the community's walls, and the holding of fairs. The monks were ordered to remain within the walls of the monastery and to dine regularly together. But a fire broke out which nearly burnt the commissioner alive in his bed, and did much damage. Layton's reaction was immediate and revealed his true concern; the flames would destroy the shrine. He reported to Cromwell on his action: 'As soon as I had set men to quench the fire I went into the church and set four monks with ban dogs to keep the shrine and put the sexton in the vestry to keep the jewels, appointing monks in every quarter of the church with candles. Also I sent for the abbot of St Augustine's to be in readiness to take down the shrine, and send the jewels into St Augustine's.' Three years later Mr Pollard, an officer of the Exchequer, came down for the loot from St Thomas's shrine, and a contemporary wrote sarcastically: 'Mr Pollard has been so busy night and day in prayer with offering unto St Thomas's shrine and hearse . . . that he could have no idle worldly time' for other business.

He went away with two great chests, filled with gold and precious stones, so heavy that seven strong men could do no more than convey one at a time out of the Cathedral and onto the train of waggons that soon made its way back to the royal palace. The shrine was smashed and the saint's bones burnt. Two years later the monastery surrendered to Archbishop Cranmer. The prior received a pension of £80 a year, and those monks who did not join the new Cathedral foundation, lesser sums.

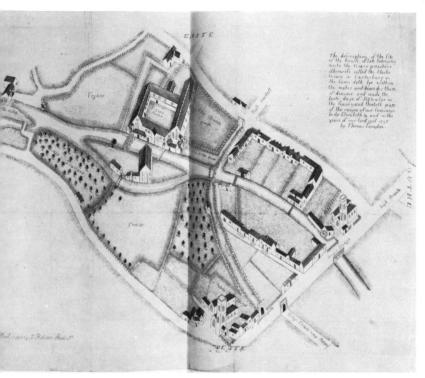

33 *An eighteenth-century plan of Black Friars, Canterbury as it would have been before its dissolution*

St Augustine's Abbey had surrendered earlier, in 1538. The abbot received a pension of £61 a year and the manor of Sturry. The aged abbot of Faversham, John Sheppey, had been earlier asked to resign by Cromwell because of his age. He had refused and had written to Cromwell in terms of remarkable dignity: 'The cheyf office and profession of an abbot is (as I have ever taken it) to lyve chaste and solytarilye, to be separate from the intromeddlynge of worldley thinge, to serve God quietlye, and to distribute his faculties in the refreshing of poor indigent persons, to have vigilant eigh to good ordre, the rule of his house, and the flock to him commytted in God.' He was allowed to stay until 1538, when he surrendered the abbey, and was granted a pension of 100 marks a year.

The friars offered Cromwell more opposition: two leaders of Canterbury Greyfriars had died at Tyburn with Elizabeth Barton, having previously done public penance at Canterbury, and the Prior of Blackfriars had been forced to flee abroad. The end of the friaries came in 1538. Their members were made, in the usual way, not only to renounce their order's property, but the very ideals of their calling.

Several religious hospitals survived the reformation, though several again had been closed before the 1530s. St John's Hospital, Northgate, in Canterbury, St Nicholas's Hospital at Harbledown, the almshouses at Hythe and at St Bartholomew's, Sandwich were allowed to continue their work for the old and sick, and today continue to do so, sensibly modernised, with a resident nurse, living tributes to one of the best parts of the monastic tradition. The Eastbridge hospital, Canterbury, retained its extensive estates. The University of Kent at Canterbury stands today on much of its land.

One important imposture was revealed, an exposure which did great harm to the monks' cause. At Boxley the monastery was famous for its celebrated Rood of Grace. On the Cross stood an image of the Virgin, which was supposed to be miraculously gifted with movement and speech, and to it pilgrims and men seeking cures had flocked for more than a century. In 1538 Geoffrey Chamber, who was pulling the Abbey down, wrote that he had found about the image certain engines and old wire, with old rotten sticks in the back, which caused the eyes to move and stir in the head thereof 'like unto a lively thing' and also the nether lip as though it should speak 'which was not a little strange to him and others present'. The day of his discovery was market day in Maidstone. Chamber rushed the image to the town and showed it to the people 'who had the matter in wondrous detestation and hatred so that if the monastery had to be defaced again they would pluck it down or burn it'. The fake was taken to London, exhibited during a sermon by the Bishop of Rochester at St Paul's Cross and burnt. The monastery went to Sir Thomas Wyatt, poet-courtier and one-time lover of Anne Boleyn.

There seems to have been little popular opposition to the dissolution, and much profitable iconoclasm. New constitutions for the cathedrals at Canterbury and Rochester were formed, and the wealth of Christ Church and St Andrew's priories transferred to the Dean and Chapter of canons which now administered them. Most monastic estates had been leased out long ago, and two-thirds of them remained in Church ownership. All that had happened was that the landlord had become a churchman—the Archbishop, say or the Dean and Chapter of Rochester, —instead of a monk. Less than one tenth of monastic lands remained in the hands of the Crown. The rest made their way into the possession of courtiers and gentry loyal to the Tudor cause. Sir Thomas Wyatt gained the friary at Aylesford as well as the abbey at Boxley. The Treasurer of the King's household, Sir Thomas Cheyney of Sheppey, was granted the great priory at Minster-in-Sheppey and the abbey at Faversham. Sir Christopher Hales did well in Canterbury. He had helped in the remodelling of the Cathedral's constitution. The King retained St Augustine's in Canterbury. The lead on the roof was melted for his use at Rochester, and much of the stone from the demolished buildings was sent to Calais for fortifications or for the construction of the new castles at Deal and Walmer. A King's house was built in the grounds of the Abbey, like those constructed in the old monastic grounds at Rochester and Dartford, and used for royal visitors as they travelled along the London Road. Elizabeth stayed there; Charles I spent a night there on his way back from Dover where he had met his young Queen, Henrietta Maria; Charles II stopped there, after he had landed on Dover beach to reclaim his kingdom at the Restoration. Often the ruins were quietly pillaged by local people. 'Adrian the Brewer' bought tiles and timber from Dover Priory for £7, whereas Thomas Portway bought 'gravestones and altar stones' from the same source for 12s. Some of the monks who did not accept the fairly generous pensions they were offered joined other religious vocations. Monks of Christ Church, or of St Andrew's Priory, Rochester, joined the staff of the new cathedrals, while others became parish priests. Some became teachers, others just faded away. When, 13 years later, Mary became Queen and talked of restoring the monasteries to the monks, she found that there was little she could do.

Much if not all of this would have passed largely unheeded by the ordinary man. In 1536 Cranmer ordered an English Bible to be placed in each church, but it seems that when ordinary people began to read it the authorities became frightened. They ordered the chaining of the Bible to the lectern, and decreed that no man other than a nobleman should possess a Bible in his own home without the priest's permission. For a while priests were allowed to marry, but the policy was soon reversed and the wives had to be hidden.

Attendance at Mass on Sunday remained compulsory and the church was the same building as ever, though occasionally statues or other images were removed, with or without official approval. Relic worship and pilgrimages were forbidden, but their practice had long been declining. Henry VIII may have become the head of the Church, but its beliefs and practices remained Catholic.

It was during the six years of Edward VI's reign (1547–53) that the Reformation reached the people. Altars, images, statues were ordered to be destroyed, though a distinction was meant to be drawn between images which were superstitiously regarded and those which were merely aids to worship. The services were in English, clergy were allowed to marry, frescoes were whitewashed, the Mass became Communion with the instruction to the people that the Body and Blood of Christ were only present symbolically, while processions and practices which had been observed for 900 years had to stop. There is a reference to 'commotions' which arose as the result of the New Religion in 1550, but otherwise the changes seem to have come in quietly and to have met with little opposition. We have been left some intimate pictures of the Reformation's progress, as seen at parish level.

At Sandhurst, near Hawkhurst and the Sussex border, a parishioner complained as early as 1548 that the Rector was not sufficiently zealous. The Cross which had headed the processions that inaugurated the Mass ever since any man could remember, and long before, was still standing on the High Altar at Easter. The church's images may have been taken down but they had not been defaced. They were standing in the vestry for any man to see. The Paschal Candle and the holy sepulchre which it traditionally lit—the equivalent at Easter of the Christmas crib—had been produced as usual, though the curate swore it was nothing to do with him. At Deal the Rector was clearly unhappy with the new ways. He confessed 'that he hath said and now doth say and affirm that in the sacrament of the altar after the words of consecration there remaineth no bread but the Body of Christ really'. The services in 1548 must have been at a stage of compromise, half in English, half in Latin, for the Rector, it was said, cheated. Whenever he came to the part of the service that was to be read in English he 'putteth on his spectacles and maketh such jerking and hemming, yet when he readeth the Latin service in the Quire he doeth it without his spectacles and readeth so distinctly and plainly that every man may hear'.

In 1553, the records begin a different story. Henry VIII's and Catherine of Aragon's daughter, Mary, was on the throne, determined to recall the old faith. Though she could do little concerning the Church lands she was determined to use the full powers of Church and State to reinstate Catholicism. A drive

34   The martrydom of Margery Polley at Tunbridge in July 1555 from a contemporary woodcut

was started to reinstate the traditional vestments and confiscated plate where they could be traced—a great problem for the parishes. Married clergy were deprived of their living, among them Cranmer's brother the Archdeacon and other canons of Canterbury. At Petham four persons were presented for 'refusing Holy Bread, Holy Water, to kiss the pax or to go in procession'. And then, in 1555, the burnings started.

The fate of 36 men and 18 women of Kent who died for their beliefs between 1555 and 1558 seems particularly shocking. None of them were people of great influence unless we count the vicars of Adisham and Rolvenden, the only two priests. They came from different parts of the county and faced interrogation, in which the nature of their belief about 'the sacrament of the Mass and the altar' was the essential question, with great courage. There is something particularly appealing about the courage of the women, of Agnes Snoth of Smarden, Anne Albright and Joan Sole of Horton, and Joan Catmer of Hythe who burnt at Canterbury in January 1556 along with John Lomas of Tenterden 'singing psalms while flames spread about their ears'. Alice Benden of Staplehurst was imprisoned in Canterbury Castle for her refusal to attend church, and then moved to another prison. Here her brother who, unlike her husband, supported her throughout her trials, tried to visit her but could not locate her. Eventually he did so, lying in a small underground cellar with hardly any light. 'He, through God's merciful will, coming thither early one morning chanced to hear her voice, as she poured out unto God her sorrowful complaints, saying the Psalms of David. And there could he no otherwise relieve her, but by putting money in a loaf of bread and sticking the same on a pole and so reached it unto her. Her lying in that prison was only upon a little short straw, between a pair of stocks and a stone wall, being allowed three farthings a day—a halfpenny bread and a farthing drink. Thus did she lie nine weeks in which she never changed her apparel, whereby she became most piteous and loathsome.'

Later she was moved to the Westgate, Canterbury, and burnt on 19 July 1557. Her fate, along with others burnt at Maidstone, Rochester, Wye and Ashford, bore witness to the fact that the new faith too had roots in the lives of ordinary people.

The only opposition to Mary in the county came before the burnings started, and seems to have been prompted by strong

35 Burning 'heretics'

objections to Mary's proposed marriage with Philip of Spain.
Sir Thomas Wyatt, whose father, as we have seen, did so well out
of the Reformation, joined a conspiracy early in 1554 with the
French and Venetian ambassadors, the Earl of Devonshire, the
Welsh Marcher lords, and some nobles in the Midlands. News of
the conspiracy was leaked, the plotters elsewhere showed their
hand too early, and Wyatt was left to go ahead on his own. He
proclaimed his rising at Maidstone on 25 January, and gathered
4,000 men. Norfolk's force sent from London to suppress the
revolt, went over to Wyatt in a manner reminiscent of Cade's
rebellion 100 years earlier. Four days later Wyatt's men camped

on Blackheath. Mary reacted promptly and bravely. She proclaimed Wyatt a traitor at the Guildhall and determined to fight. Twenty thousand men enrolled under her banner and Wyatt, thinking the opposition too strong for a head-on assault on the capital, moved up-river to Kingston. On 6 February he crossed the Thames and made a desperate night attack on London, reaching Ludgate at two in the morning of 8 February. His supporters had deserted him in large numbers and he gave himself up to execution. Forty-six of his men suffered the same fate in one day, while others were sent back to Kent for execution, so that their sufferings would duly impress the people.

When Elizabeth succeeded Mary in 1558 the injunctions of the Protestant past were repeated and the drive to remove from the parish churches the sights and practices of the Catholic centuries reached a successful climax. Indeed the parishioners seem to have believed that they were called upon to perform acts of vandalism which Archbishop Parker, the new archbishop, deplored. At Bearsted, for instance, near Maidstone, 'It is presented that the glass windows in the chancel chapel and in the church be undefaced; the footstools of stone that the idols stood on be undefaced; the place where the priest did sit on festival days is undefaced; the hole where the sepulchre was wont to lie is undefaced; the steps in the chancel be standing; the Holy Water stock is undefaced; the place where the cruet stood to wash his hands(!) be undefaced.'

Fortunately other parishioners do not seem to have felt that such wholesale desecration was called for. The Elizabethan Church established itself without much difficulty. There was little opposition, and what there was received merciful treatment. Nicholas Harpsfield, Mary's main agent in the county and the man immediately responsible for the burnings, was imprisoned in the Tower till his death in 1575. Sixteen clergy were deprived of their livings for refusing to accept the new Church and in 1570, after the Pope had formally excommunicated Elizabeth, 274 parishes were inspected. Only 113 adults were described as irregular churchgoers. The same number again attended church but did not take Communion. A few old Kentish families remained loyal to the old religion. William Roper, Sir Thomas More's beloved son-in-law, was brought before the Council for his convictions in 1568, while his son Thomas was imprisoned in the Fleet 13 years later. The profound and uniquely appropriate English of the Prayer Book from now on was to be heard Sunday after Sunday by the great majority of Kentishmen until the middle of the nineteenth century.

6

Kent from Sixteenth to Eighteenth Centuries

It was typical of Kent, up to the end of the Middle Ages, that if change occurred it did so slowly, and this characteristic remained until nineteenth-century industrialisation. From the early Tudor years, despite the introduction of new crops, new wealth, new peoples bringing new industries, new threats of invasion and two civil wars, the county remained basically the same until the spread of modern industry and the size of suburban London overwhelmed much of the county, and radically altered its way of life. The agricultural life combined with the large number of small county towns which served its needs, the widespread ownership of land, the presence of the Church as an influence both spiritually and economically, the large amount of woodland, the increasing pull of London as a market, the influence of the gentry coupled with the absence of a servile mass of agricultural labourers totally dependent on landlords and farmers—these remain at the centre of Kentish life throughout the sixteenth, seventeenth and eighteenth centuries.

To say this of Kent is not to present a picture of a static society, the reverse is true. Population rose steadily from about 90,000 at the time of Elizabeth's accession to 150,000 a hundred years later, and over 300,000 in 1801—the year of the first official census. Kent was thought of as one of England's most populated counties with a high proportion—up to a third in the seventeenth century—living in its 30 'considerable towns'. Its people move about a great deal internally, from surrounding countryside to country towns or, in north-west Kent, into the capital. Immigrant communities from France, Belgium and Holland settled in Canterbury, Sandwich and Maidstone, and we find their influence strongly

106

36 'I happened to look up and was quite astonished to perceive cows grazing upon a spot apparently 50 feet above the tops of the houses.' (William Cobbett, Rural Rides . . .)

championed by their Kentish neighbours when it came under attack, as it was, for religious reasons, by Archbishop Laud. New ideas as well as new farming and industrial techniques entered the county along the London–Dover road in the same way as they have always done. Yet the changes were readily assimilated. The Kent which the poet Sir Thomas Wyatt knew and which Defoe described, is not so very different from the county through which William Cobbett rode in September 1823, and which he surveyed from a hill near Hollingbourne on his way to Maidstone:

'When I got to the edge of the hill, and before I got off my horse to lead him down this more than mile of hill, I sat and surveyed the prospect before me, and to the right and to the left. This is what the people of Kent call the *Garden of Eden*. It is a district of meadows, corn fields, hop-gardens, and orchards of apples, pears, cherries and filberts with very little if any land which cannot, with propriety, be called good. There are plantations of chestnut and of ash frequently occurring: and as these are cut when long enough to make poles for hops, they are at all times objects of great beauty.'

To read Cobbett's account of Dover after a visit to its modern streets, throbbing with frustrated continental lorries, is to realize how far we have travelled ourselves from his landscape: 'I got into Dover rather late. It was dusk when I was going down the street towards the quay. I happened to look up, and was quite astonished to perceive cows grazing upon a spot apparently 50 feet above the tops of the houses, and measuring horizontally not, perhaps, more than 20 feet from a line which would have formed a continuation into the air.'

Kent has been one of England's most visited counties, and the fact that visitors naturally stick to the beaten path must put one on one's guard. A tourist's view is always limited, and the sheer size of the county makes one realize that an account such as that given by Thomas Baskerville, a Berkshire man, after the Restoration, describes not Kent so much as the view seen from Watling Street: 'It is one of the best-cultivated counties of any in England and great part of my way that I went to Dover being through delicious orchards of cherries, pears and apples, and great hop-gardens. In husbandry affairs they are very neat binding up all sorts of grain in sheaves; they give the best wages to labourers of any in England, in harvest giving four and five shillings for an acre of wheat and two shillings a day meat and drink, which doth invite many stout workmen hither from the neighbouring country to get in their harvest.'

Such an account could not have been made of Romney Marsh, for instance, where the population declined by about one third in between 1570 and 1670, as it became the property of absentee graziers whose flocks were tended by overlookers, nor of the Thames or Sheppey marshland. The heavy wet soil of the Weald, with its high proportion of woodland, would not have produced a picture of such a smiling scene. Yet that Kent was, compared to the rest of the country, prosperous and that its prosperity was fairly widely spread is clearly a generalisation that was accepted by Kentishmen and visitors alike.

Long before the end of the Middle Ages serfdom had vanished in Kent, and the people of the county lived a variety of lives which are most satisfactorily difficult to docket. About two or three per cent of the seventeenth-century population were gentlemen, whose income was largely drawn from farm rents and from the profits of their home farms. But though they were the accepted leaders of their communities, providing from one generation to the next the county's members of parliament and dominating the magistrates' bench, they did not possess the vast estates and the unchallenged power over their tenantry which made so much of English life still feudal centuries after feudalism had died in the history books. Another one or two per cent were clergy, the most influential of whom came from county families and merged easily into the gentry. The remaining 95 per cent were a bewildering variety of farmers of all sorts, of farm labourers, some owning a small holding or spending much of each year at sea, others living in their farmers' houses, as dependent upon them as any domestic servant, of country shopkeepers who were just as much countrymen as any farmer, and of labourers in the dockyard towns of Deptford and Chatham who took the summer months off to help with the harvest on their families' farms. It was a genuinely mixed society, even if also one of cohesion and stability.

County society was led by two or three dozen families most of whom had been long established in Kent and were intimately connected with each other. In 1648, when a formidable rising against the rule of Parliament was organised by the gentry, particularly in central and east Kent, the cry was, 'For God, King Charles and Kent'. By appealing in this manner to the county's traditional independence the gentry showed how deeply involved in purely local affairs they were, an involvement which was the basis of their strength in their own communities. Most of them had taken little part in the first civil war of 1642–45, and the county as a whole had shared their lack of interest in the great political and social upheaval that was occurring in the capital. But by 1648 Kent had had enough of irregular taxation, of insults to the established church, of the growing challenge not just to the policies of the Crown but to the monarchical system itself, and people followed their social superiors, if only momentarily, to arms. Later they were to relapse into a stubborn and unobtrusive non-resistance, when the power of the Commonwealth and Protectorate proved too much for them, an attitude which was to change to open enthusiasm for the returned Charles II when he rode from Dover into Canterbury across the Barham Downs, in the spring of 1660. Proximity to the capital had little effect on social and political attitudes, so that Kent remained stubbornly parochial, despite the traffic on the London–Dover Road, showing, like the wild red deer of Holmesdale, that 25 miles distance from London was enough to form a world apart. It was said that Kentish dialects in Tudor times were incomprehensible to those who came from without the county, but the gentry could understand them easily enough and probably shared them, if in a

37 *A Victorian reconstruction of a Medieval banquet in the Great Hall of Penshurst Place*

modified form.

The houses of the gentry grew out of the Kentish past, generation by generation, like the life of the people. There are few examples of great houses, built, like Blenheim Palace, all of a piece, the result of a single architect's vision, carried through to the bankrupted end in defiance of obstacles and the interests of local people. There is Mereworth Castle, it is true, halfway between Maidstone and Tonbridge, where a whole village, castle and church were razed to build an eighteenth-century Palladian house with a dome like that of St Paul's Cathedral. But far more common, among the county's great houses, is the gradual development summed up by Professor Alan Everitt: 'The typical pattern of domestic architecture in Kent consisted of a Saxon or Norman site, a mediaeval building with Tudor accretions and Jacobean embellishments.'[1]

The houses grew too out of the local area. Much of Canterbury Cathedral may have been built of Caen stone and Henry VIII's forts at Deal and Walmer from materials pillaged from the monasteries, but Penshurst and Hever were built of local sandstone, Knole from stone quarried in the park, and Broome made from the master's own brick kilns. As Professor Everitt puts it: '. . . The manor-houses of Kentish families were rarely the elegant "gentlemen's seats" of a later age, set in the countryside, but not truly of it. Each was a genuine farmhouse as well as a manorial hall, the centre of its parish or community, a microcosm of rural society.'[2]

The gentry, though united by pride of ancestry and gentle status, varied greatly in wealth. They ranged from the richest of them all, the earls of Thanet, members of the Tufton family, whose seventeenth-century income was about £10,000 a year, to the most impoverished whose income was £100 a year. Many of the 'middling-sized' gentry would own estates worth £400 to £1,000 a year. In the north-west of the county there was a steady arrival of courtiers, merchants and lawyers from the capital but in general the gentry stayed fiercely Kentish, 60 per cent of their seventeenth-century wives and husbands being born in the county. Many had profited from the sale of monastic lands or from that of the Crown estates which went on steadily from the Tudor period. They spent nearly all their life on their estates, and had little time or inclination for London life. Improvement and extension of the

[1] Alan Everitt, *Community of Kent and the Great Rebellion*, p. 30.
[2] *Op. cit.*, p. 29.

family estate meant success, its sale out of the family, the ultimate failure. Dr Chalklin quotes a charming letter from Edwin Stede whose father had been forced to sell Stede Hill in Harrietsham about 1660. He is writing to his brother: 'I am much troubled that the estate that has soe long borne our name and family and our ancestors bones should be tumbled about and disturbed to make room for those of strangers.'[3]

The years of civil wars and of the Protectorate from 1640 to 1660 brought with them high taxation or even sequestration of estates, if the family was openly Royalist, but rebuilding and improvements of Kentish country houses started again with the Restoration. Slave trade money seems to have found its way to Squerryes, Westerham, as well as Stede Hill, for Sir Nicholas Crispe, who rebuilt it in 1681, was the son of a wealthy Guinea merchant. Some Kentish gentry lived in medieval castles, like the Culpepers at Leeds, though Sir Dudley Digges who helped to promote the Petition of Right let his keep at Chilham fall into ruins—considered fashionable in the next century when Capability Brown landscaped the grounds—and built a Jacobean house alongside it. Others like Sir William Selby who adapted Ightham Mote lived

[3] This material, along with much more in this chapter, is drawn from Dr C. W. Chalklin's *Seventeenth-Century Kent* (1965).

38 *Igtham Mote*

in moated manor houses, dating from the later Middle Ages, when wealthy men longed to build houses and not barracks, but felt they must still be protected. But the most popular were the 'hall houses' built, like the yeomen's houses, round a central hall with a high beamed roof, from which service rooms, parlours, and bedrooms led off. The finest of all such halls stands still unaltered at Penshurst Place, with its great carved wooden figures of farm workers leaning inwards on either side of the medieval chestnut raftered roof. In the Great Hall at Knole, originally a late medieval building, the Elizabethan Thomas Sackville, first Earl of Dorset, a member of the Boleyn family and a cousin of the Queen's, installed an elaborate plaster ceiling, oak panelling and a fantastically carved wooden screen, with a musician's gallery above in which his private orchestra of ten played during meals. These were eaten by his whole household, seated at separate tables. On the raised platform at the end of the hall sat the earl, his lady, his children, and his guests. In the main body of the hall the

39   *Knole, Sevenoaks*

members of the household sat at different tables according to their occupations, among which there would be the Kitchen table, probably the largest, the Nursery table, the Clerks' table, and the Laundrymaids' table.

By the seventeenth century most halls had generally been chambered over, and divided into bedrooms with a staircase leading from the old hall. Wainscoting—panelling—of rooms was very popular. At Great Maydeken in Barham Henry Oxinden kept a record of his work. In 1633 the 'great stairs' were 'builded and seeled', 'harthplaces' were built and windows inserted in the parlours and chambers at a cost of £63.5.3*d*. In 1640 he did some wainscoting, and again the next year he was wainscoting 'my studie and the cabanet over itt'. He also 'new birthed the room over the kitchin, the chamber over the little parlour, sealed itt, made the partition to the closett in itt, wainscotted and shelved itt, and laid the wall of the said chamber in a greene colour'.

The head of a county family lived an industrious and responsible life. All its members, including those from the many minor

40   *A Tudor interior :*
Stoneacre near Maidstone

branches which would occupy lesser houses in the county, deferred to him while he in return regarded every member of the family, including poor relations and those temporarily on hard times, as part of his responsibility. In addition he would help and entertain the local poor, and provide as much work in his house or on his estate as his finances would allow. Sir George Sondes, Sheriff of Kent in the 1630s, claimed that his house was always open to all comers. He provided relief to 20 poor people a week, on average, while his household consumed a 50 stone bullock a week, and a barrel of beer a day. He held family prayers once or twice a day and attended Church twice on Sundays with his servants. His work as a Justice of the Peace, either sitting to hear cases in his own home, or in company with his fellow magistrates at Maidstone or at Canterbury, would occupy much of a gentleman's time and attention, if he was at all conscientious. Sir Edward Dering's notebook for 1633 describes the cases which came before him often in his own home at Surrenden Dering or in the house of a fellow justice. Such business took up four or five days a month and included the granting of licences to victuallers, making a bastardy order, fining absentees from Church, mending highways, apprenticing pauper children, and enforcing the Act of 1589 which aimed to prevent the building of cottages without four acres of land, an act which must surely have stood rather as a pious hope than a statement of policy to be implemented. This was the 'rule of the gentry' and it was to stay, essentially unchallenged, until the labourer's revolt of 1830 and the rise of the nineteenth-century state.

Kent was, however, famous for its yeomen, or small farmers,

41   *A Tudor yeoman's house: Lynsted Court*

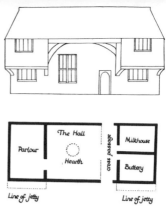

Parlour

The Hall

○
Hearth

cross passage

Milkhouse

Buttery

Line of jetty   *Line of jetty*

whether tenant or free, rather than its gentry. During these centuries their houses, timber-framed at first though later built more frequently of brick, appeared in large numbers all over the county, especially in the Weald, and still stand today, typically Kentish, the homes of farmers, professional people or, increasingly, London commuters. The size of their farms and their incomes varied enormously. Some of them farmed no more than five or ten acres; the Wealden holdings were particularly small. Here the income might be as low as £20 a year. Others might draw more than £200 a year from farms of over 100 acres, and lived lives indistinguishable from those of the gentry, even marrying into their families like Katherine Cullinge of Barham who married her neighbour Henry Oxinden in 1642. Generally the county's custom of gavelkind inheritance which was followed by the yeomen farmers if the owner died intestate, but not by the gentry, led to the splitting up of farms and their consequently permanently small acreage. But, whether their holdings were large or small, they were all entitled, as 40 shilling freeholders, to cast their votes in the elections for Kentish members of parliament held in the open on Penenden Heath near Maidstone—presuming that they could get themselves there—and the gentry were unlikely to forget this power.

Their houses, like those of the gentry, were based on a central hall built of local materials, and grew steadily over the generations. By 1600 the original open hearth was replaced by a brick fireplace with a brick chimney stack, placed at one end of the hall. The stack would also serve the kitchen fireplace built on the other side of the hall's wall. At the other end of the hall the farmer's bed chamber was built on. Meals, as at Knole or Penshurst, were eaten in common in the hall, the maids and resident farm workers sitting down with the farmer's family. By the seventeenth century

117

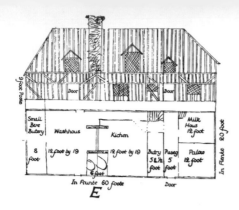

the high halls of these houses had also been chambered over though often the rooms on the first floor would be used for storing corn or malt, rather than just as bedrooms, for the 'hall-house' was very much of a working concern. Around the chimney stack in Tudor times was built the staircase,—a great improvement on the old ladder—and in the walls of the upstairs rooms were inserted dormer windows to let in the light, though the little leaded panes reduced their efficiency. At the side of the house— probably next to the kitchens—outhouses would proliferate. There would be a wash-house with a proper water supply— something which in south-east England was said to be known only to Kent—a bakehouse, a buttery, a milk-house and perhaps a brew house. Life was growing more comfortable, as the eighteenth century approached.

The difference in comfort and social ease of different farmers can be seen in the inventories of furniture which were drawn up for two different men, both of whom died in 1602. John Blaxland of Northbourne, near Deal, left a table in the hall, a bench, two forms and two stools, a cupboard containing pots and pans, tableware of pewter and wood and fire-irons for the hearth. The bedroom, which was at one end of the hall and was the room in which he died, contained a feather-bed and bedsteads, two chairs, two chests, a table, and a good stock of linen, including nine pairs of sheets. The three chambers on the upper floor, contained one feather-bed and furniture worth a mere £1.10s. At the other end of the county in the Isle of Sheppey Richard Askew of Minster was far more prosperous. His hall contained four tables, 12 stools, and four chairs, a picture of a ship on the wall and six scutcheons of arms, which would make one think he had social ambitions. He left a fine store of pewter ware, and a magnificent four poster bed, with green say curtains, valued at £4 15s 4d. His parlour contained a small picture, 'three chayers seated and backetted with leather, very old', two window 'quishines' and six other cushions, though there were no floor carpets. Eighty years later at Eythorne, again near Deal, John Marsh died worth £347 4s 6d. The best bedroom, now upstairs, contained a bed, cupboard, three chests, a trunk, and a pair of coal irons. The parlour, which here meant a living room, though often it signified a bedroom, was furnished with tables, stools, chairs, a cupboard and fire-irons. Its pewter exceeded £5 in value, its silver £3. The hall seems to have been used as a kitchen, since it contained a spit, dripping pan, and two dozen trenchers, but it must also have been used as another living room, for it contained tables, chairs, and desks. The linen was worth £12 12s.

Tiling came in steadily during the sixteenth century. The faded medley of reds, pinks, fawns and browns of Kentish roofs now formed increasingly the roofscape of the county's towns and villages, and provides a major ingredient in their beauty today. As the seventeenth century progressed, more and more of the wooden frames and plaster work—often the top half only of the farmhouses—were bricked over or, even more typically Kentish, tile-hung. Extra rooms, for servants or guests, were added, or first floor store rooms converted into bedrooms, their contents moved either upstairs again, in the new attics that became the next development in house conversion, or to further outhouses at the back or side of the house. Often, if the house belonged to a craftsman, a weaver, for instance, or a carpenter, one of the rooms was used as the shop. Later again, as in the house where the author was partly brought up, a front room overlooking the village street was used as another sort of shop from which the trader—in this case a butcher—sold his wares.

Over the years, from the sixteenth to the eighteenth centuries, life became more comfortable for the yeomen, as the increasing length of the inventories of their wills shows. At first only basic needs for leisure and refreshment were met. The most valuable piece of furniture was the best bed, either feather or flock, according to wealth, with its hangings. Clothes were stored in chests, there would be stools around the table but little else to sit on, cupboards, in which household goods were stacked, were open, though perhaps a cloth might be hung in front of them. But there seems to have been plenty of sheets, towels, 'pillowcotes' (pillowcases) and blankets, with pewter plates and pots and dishes. The kitchen was well stocked with cooking utensils too as was that of Thomas Halsnode of Biddenden who died in 1570:

'Item in yron worke, 2 spitts, 2 tryvetts (kettle stands over a fire), a brande yron, a grydyron, a freynge panne prised at   6s. 8d.
Item in latten (brass) 4 candlesticks   20d.
Item in brasse a cawdren, 3 little keatells and a brass pott and an yron pott prised at   26s. 8d.
Item in wodden vessells, bowles, dyshess, and trenchars with such smale tryvells at.'   20d.

One receives the impression that life was work, and food—quite good food—and sleep. Careful provision was made for widows, or other dependents, who would continue to occupy the house and whose interests might well be brushed aside. They were given a room of their own, and right of access to the only fire in the hall.

By the early eighteenth century many farmhouses saw more spacious lives. The painted canvas wall hangings which adorned the walls—if anything hid the plaster and beams—gave way to panelling. The parlour had become a sitting room for the family away from the servants, the hall had become the kitchen, clothes were stored in chests of drawers, clocks ticked away the long hours. It was the same life, but with some refinements.

Separate again from the yeoman, with a way of life and work, that merged into his as the yeoman's merged into that of the gentry, was the husbandman, a small-holder who worked for a richer farmer at certain times of year, such as ploughing or harvest, to supplement his income from his own land. Some were no better off than labourers, with personal estates worth £15 or less. Others lived in the style of a yeoman farmer. Generally their

44 *A smallholding at Hoo, c. 1740*

houses were smaller with less rooms built onto or above the hall, flock instead of feather beds, only occasional hangings or cushions, less pots and pans, fewer pewter plates and 'sawsers' and old furniture of low valuation. Country craftsmen, such as blacksmiths, wheelwrights and carpenters, lived like the husbandmen, but some country shopkeepers—grocers for instance—might rather resemble the yeoman.

The proportion of labourers to farmers varied from one part of the county to another. In the Weald it seems that each occupied about one-third of the population, the remainder being mainly occupied by tradespeople or craftsmen. In the north of the county, where the supply of corn for the London market led it to be called the granary of the capital, there was a higher proportion of labourers. The same was true of east Kent, where at the beginning of the nineteenth century Cobbett is blasting off typical broadsides at the poverty of areas dominated by a few large corn farmers, whose labourers live always on the poverty line. At Ash-next-Sandwich in 1705 there were 59 people who were described as farmers out of a population of 363. The great majority of the remainder were labourers, either resident or non-resident.

Resident labourers like domestic servants were generally unmarried, and entered into a contract for a particular period—a quarter, say, or a half year, some for a year—often to undertake a particular job. The account-books of Sir Roger Twysden, whose estate was at Royden Hall, East Peckham, show these annual wages in the middle of the seventeenth century:

Women servants—50 shillings
Nurse   —£5
Cook   —£5
Ploughman   —£6
Boy-gardener   —50 shillings

They were given full board and lodging and lived with the gentleman or more often, the farmer, eating with him, though, as we have seen, the practice was growing less common as the years went by. Their food and room—such as it was, and it must have often been no more than a rough bed in a store room along with other farm workers—was worth about £8–£10 a year. There was little question of poverty among resident labourers, though they lived a life of dependence which is difficult to associate with the continual claims about the independence of Kentishmen which we hear from medieval times onwards. It was among the married 'out' labourers that the cases of hardship were found. Here a labourer would earn between £12 to £18 a year if fully employed, but such employment was rare. Many labourers would only gain work for 150–200 days a year at an average of a shilling a day. Their families must have lived permanently on subsistence level, with the head of the household often paid by the piece, or contracted for by the job—one shilling a score, for instance, for shearing, 5d a rod for hedging, 1/6d an acre for mowing. But even among the labourers Kent's wages were regarded as among the highest in the country, for London, as always, paid higher rates, as did work in the dockyards or on the fishing boats, and the labourer's pay was raised, even if not by much, through this competition. And, as always, class merged into class. In Thanet small farmers and labourers and fishermen worked two jobs. The mackerel fishing began in May when the barley sowing had ended. The herring fishing would not start until the harvest was completed, and would end when the autumn sowing of wheat began in November.

The labourer's cottages were small, at the most not more than two or three rooms—hall, bed chamber, and kitchen. At Chartham we know of a house which consisted of just a hall and a loft above it, and there may have been cottages of only one room. Fortunately, if one can make so brutal a statement, the families were small. It has been calculated that amongst the population of the county as a whole about half the children born died before they were 16, and the proportion would be highest, as always, among the poor. The plague—mainly a scourge of the towns— smallpox, influenza, and tuberculosis brought on by cramped ill-ventilated housing were mainly responsible; it was rare to find a big family of children. The picture we have of large numbers of ragged, dirty, desperately undernourished, children spilling out of farm labourers' front doors derives from Victorian times. In Ash-next-Sandwich in 1705 only ten families out of 270 had more than five children, and none more than eight. The average was a little under two. Furnishings were very simple to judge from the probate inventories—flockbeds, pillows, some sheets and blankets, pewter plates, pots and pans, some chests, a table and forms. Many labourers had hardly any animals, and even less land. The four acres of land which were to be attached to cottages built after the 1589 act do not seem to have materialised. But few of them turned to relief, because, no doubt, they knew very well they would never be granted it unless they were unable to work or had some exceptional need. At Ash, at the beginning of the eighteenth century, about one in nine of the people was receiving alms, but they were the old, the widowed, or the sick. At Headcorn, in the Weald, there were 13 cases of help listed for the approval of the parish meeting in the year 1700. Five were widows or widowers, one was an orphaned couple of boys, one was 'underwitted', one a 'dumb girl aged 19, and hath had relief 12 years', another a lame man, three had large families and seem to have been helped by the parish in the form of family allowances, and one an elderly couple, aged 76 and 69. If you were fit and out of food, or work, or money you sought it where you could—rabbits, perhaps, or larks, the 'four and twenty blackbirds baked in a pie', the produce of your garden if you had one—or went without. But as always when one tries to reconstruct the life of working people one is trying to reconstruct a jig-saw puzzle most of whose pieces have been lost. Few farm labourers left wills and most of their cottages have been destroyed. They made their way into documents only when they sought poor relief.

Many of the rural poor moved into the towns—often no more than a single street with fields running up to the back gardens—where, particularly if the area was thriving, more work was to be gained. But town life did not provide much opportunity for unskilled labour. Most of the workers were craftsmen. Seventy per cent of little Tonbridge's population were tradesmen or craftsmen. Elsewhere skilled men, serving a wealthy professional class of great discrimination, were to be found in larger numbers—goldsmiths and silversmiths at Canterbury, bookbinders and clockmakers at Tunbridge Wells or Greenwich, where a population of retired middle-class Londoners was developing. Chatham, Rochester, and Deptford were thriving dockyard towns, among the only seven county towns with a population of over 2,500 inhabitants according to a church census of 1676. Already, when Defoe described them in the 1720s, the Medway towns were beginning to run into one another and the complexity of activity he saw there impressed him: 'The building-yards, docks, timber-yard, deal-yard, mast-yard, gun-yard, rope-walks and all the other

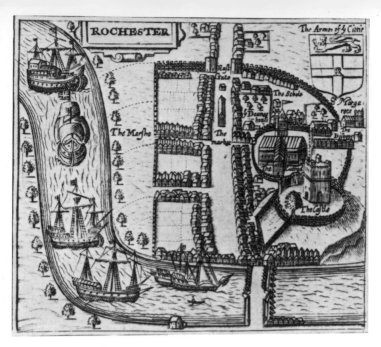

yards and places, set apart for the works belonging to the navy, are
like a well-ordered city; and though you see the whole place as it
were in the utmost hurry, yet you see no confusion, every man
knows his own business. . . .'

By the beginning of the seventeenth century Chatham had
surpassed the older Woolwich and Deptford yards, and had
become the country's main naval dockyard. Its population rose
from one thousand in 1600 to five thousand a century later. The
expansion created a large demand for local materials and craftsmen and the area boomed, though, like all areas dependent on a
permanent state of war or preparation for war for its prosperity,
it suffered terribly when naval building programmes were cut
back, or governments failed to meet their commitments. In the
early days of the bankrupt Charles I, for instance, shipwrights and
other craftsmen marched to London demanding the one year's
wages and half a year's board which was owed them. After the
Dutch wars of his elder son's reign men were laid off in their
hundreds, and a few years after his younger son's flight into exile
800 men were reported to be too weak to work. They were starv-
ing, since their pay was in arrears.

Chatham's hard wood came mainly from Kent's forests
particularly in the Weald. Here the roads were so bad, and the

soil so heavy, that the great teams of horses and oxen could take months to deliver their loads to the yards, as they strained and heaved their wheels out of ruts in which a man could easily drown. Towards the end of the eighteenth century Hasted describes the roads near Tenterden, as being 'so miry, that the traveller's horse frequently plunges through them up to the girths of the saddle . . .' There is an account of 1600 which claims it took two years to carry timber from woods near Tonbridge to the Chatham yards. Defoe had the same experience 100 years later. The loads were left by the roadside, where they had stuck, during the winter, to be taken up again when the roads dried. The ropes, sails, and anchors would be made in the yards while Kent would supply most of the bricks and tiles and some of the guns. The gunpowder industry at Faversham expanded under the navy's demand. Deal and Tunbridge Wells were the only new towns in the county to emerge in the seventeenth century. Celia Fiennes, who paid a quick visit there in 1697, was impressed with the contrast between the newly developed Deal, which existed to serve the area of the Channel close to the Downs, where ships would anchor as they left or entered the Thames estuary, and the old town of Sandwich, which the sea had left during Elizabeth's reign, despite the city's elaborate hospitality to that Queen, expended in the unfulfilled hope that her government would take steps to prevent the silting up of its harbour, as it had done so successfully in the case of Dover: 'Deal looks like a good thriving place, the buildings new and neat brickwork with gardens. I believe they are most masters of ships houses and seamen or else that belong to the cordage and sail making, with other requisites to shipping . . .'

Contrast this cheery sight with Sandwich: 'This is a sad old town all timber building, you enter by a gate and so you go out of it by a gate, but it's run so to decay that except one or two good houses it's just like to drop down the whole town.' In any event, there most of those houses still stand today forming one of the most beautiful country towns in England, despite its appalling traffic problems.

Tunbridge Wells was a special kind of town, if town it could be called—a spa which like the later seaside towns of the nineteenth and twentieth centuries, was full for the season, which lasted from May till October, but emptied during the winter months. The origin of its prosperity would appear to lie in the drunkenness which was fashionable, if not mandatory, at James I's court. In the summer of 1606 Lord North, who had been advised to seek country air after his debauched life at court, was staying with his friend Lord Abergavenny at Eridge Park, on the Kent–Sussex border. He passed a spring in a wood, on his journey home, and drank some of its water which was offered to him by a cottager. It reminded him of medicinal springs he knew in Germany, and took samples of the water, which was full of iron, back with him to London. He returned the next year for a course of the waters, claimed to be much the better for them—whether or not he also moderated his drinking we are not told—and publicised his good fortune among his friends at court. In 1630 Queen Henrietta Maria visited the Wells for six weeks after Charles II's birth, and

46   *Tunbridge Wells in the early 18th century*

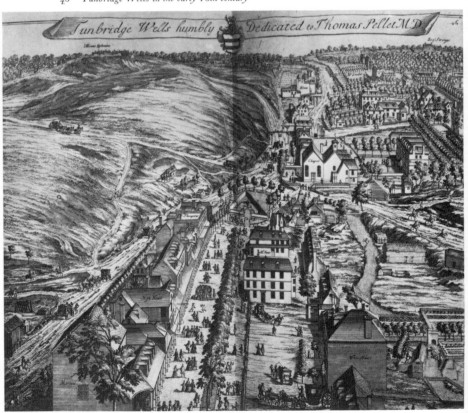

declared herself 'much improved in health'. The reputation of the spa was now assured.

When Celia Fiennes visited the Wells, in 1697 she found the atmosphere informal, and the classes, like the sexes, mixing freely, an experience she savoured, despite its dangers: 'You engage with the Ladies at play without any introduction . . . every Gentleman is equally received by the Fair Sex upon the Walks. This indistinction is attended with one inconvenience that Sharpers, whose trade is to go Genteel . . . mix themselves in all the diversions . . .'

Formal dinners were not eaten, and the pleasures of shopping in the open markets were enjoyed by the sophisticated, a practice which leads the diarist on to one of her most breathless sentences: 'All people buy their own provision at the market, which is just by the Wells and furnished with great plenty of all sorts flesh, fowl, and fish in great plenty is brought from Rye and Deal etc., this being the road to London, so all the season the water is drank they stop here which makes it very cheap, as also the Country people come with all their back yard and barn door affords, to supply them with, and their gardens and orchards which makes the markets well stored and provision cheap, which the gentry takes as a diversion while drinking the waters to go and buy their dinners it being every day's market and runs the whole length of the walk. . . .'

Defoe visited Tunbridge Wells in the next generation, and seems also to have been pleased with his stay. He arrived, by chance, at the same time as the Prince of Wales, and like Celia Fiennes, was struck by the quantity of 'gaming, sharping, intriguing, as also fops, fools, beaux, and the like . . .' But, granted one essential, the Wells was a fine town for 'a man of character and good behaviour': 'In a word, Tunbridge wants nothing that can add to the felicities of life, or that can make a man or woman completely happy, always provided they have money; for without money a man is nobody at Tunbridge, any more than at any other place; and when any man finds his pockets low, he has nothing left to think of but to be gone, for he will have no diversion in staying there any longer.'

In the next generation again, Tunbridge Wells reached the height of its fame during the 26 years from 1735 when 'Beau' Nash ruled its life as Master of Ceremonies. Nash laid down a code of public conduct which all were obliged to follow. The social rough

47   *Tunbridge Wells in 1748—at the height of its popularity*

and tumble described by Celia Fiennes became a thing of the past and during 'King' Nash's rule, virtually every well-known man in the country visited the Wells, where his life followed a strict pattern. He would rise early, and take the waters between seven and nine in the morning. After breakfast he would go to church, and fill up the rest of the morning walking, talking or gossiping. Dinner would be taken in his lodging where the company would change into formal dress for the afternoon's parade along the Walks (the modern Pantiles). The evening would be spent in the Assembly Rooms, dancing, gambling, tea-drinking, and indefatigably gossiping between times, until the day closed about 11 p.m. The earlier ironic remark of Defoe's strikes even truer of the Nash period: '. . . Those people who have nothing to do anywhere else seem to be the only people who have anything to do at Tunbridge.'

With Nash's departure, and the later rise of Brighton which was greatly helped by the improvement of the London–Brighton Road, Tunbridge Wells's day as the centre of the fashionable world, second only to Bath, was ended.

Canterbury still had the largest population of the county's

towns at the end of the seventeenth century, though Deptford, with about 7,000 people, was running it close. The city had received a shot in the arm in the previous century, as a result of the Protestant persecutions in the Low Countries—mainly in the part we call Belgium—and in France. During the Spanish persecutions in Flanders, groups of skilled craftsmen, chiefly Calvinist cloth-workers, left the Low Countries for England, encouraged by Elizabeth's government and, it would appear, tolerated (even, on occasion, welcomed) by the insular Kentishmen, so long as they did not undertake work which directly competed with that of local people. There were nearly 1,000 foreigners in seventeenth-century Canterbury, where Huguenots, after the massacre of St Bartholomew in 1570, had joined the Flemish. They were mainly cloth-workers and silk-weavers and though Canterbury was glad enough to have the new men, manufacturing the 'new draperies', Cranbrook suffered from their enterprise. For they manufactured cloth which was lighter than the traditional heavy broad cloth, and was in much demand in Europe. The old Blackfriars building became their Weavers' Hall while the Huguenots were given the Norman Crypt under the Cathedral, where Becket's remains had been buried after his murder. Archbishop Laud tried to close down the Huguenot church, and was surprised to find the citizens of Canterbury rising so warmly to their defence. But here Celia Fiennes still found them at the end of the seventeenth century, when there had been a further round of immigration following Louis xiv's revocation of the edict of Nantes in 1685, and here the Huguenot community still meets today.

By the time she saw their chapel, the prosperity of the clothing industry had suffered from East Anglian competition, and silk-weaving had taken its place. When Defoe visited the city in 1720 silk-weaving had given place to hops, as a basis for Canterbury's prosperity.

Sandwich, too had been pleased to welcome the immigrants. Elizabeth may have refused the £10,000 necessary for the new outlet to the sea the city needed, but her government issued an invitation in 1561 to Flemish master workers in baize and flannels to settle, and the first 25 came that year. Later Dutch settlers left their mark on the town whose houses, like those of their counterparts in Topsham, Devon, can be easily distinguished. They did

not confine themselves to the cloth trade. The Flemings were the market gardeners of Europe, and the fields around Sandwich, many of which were reclaimed by the Flemings and still bear the name of 'polder' today, were growing carrots, cabbages, celery, flax, and seeds for sale in the London market, by the beginning of the seventeenth century.

Other immigrant craftsmen settled in Maidstone, where they established a thriving linen industry. Maidstone's importance had been obvious over the Civil War period, not just because of the battle which was fought there, but because of the way it had become a focus for political opinion in the county. The gentry met there for the Assizes and concerted policy; the Kentish Petition of 1642 was drawn up at the Star Inn, while the county freeholders cast their votes at election times on Penenden Heath, nearby. Defoe loved the place, for it contained 'persons of figure and quality . . . where a man of letters and of manners will always find suitable society both to divert and improve himself'. He came to it via Gravesend, Rochester, Sheerness and Faversham and found the change in scenery and social class much to his liking.

Of the ports, Margate and Ramsgate had overtaken Dover by the beginning of the eighteenth century. Both ports grew up on the coastal trade in coal from the north-east of England, an expanding business as industry began to demand more and more coal and the roads could not carry the loads, except by packhorse, lump by lump. Overseas trade was important to Dover but to few other county ports. It was internal trade which employed the great majority of the seamen, who formed one in 30 of Kent's male workers. Above all they throve on trade with London, the great national magnet, whose population had grown from 50,000 in the early sixteenth century to over 500,000 by the end of the seventeenth. Little ships, less than 100 tons, carried the goods and passengers to London which the roads could not cope with, and returned with holds full of largely British goods for the people of their area. Margate, Faversham, and Rochester also took a large part in carrying corn, while in addition Faversham exported most of the county's wool—again to London. London's timber, much of it cut in the north of the county, was carried in barges from Erith and Woolwich. Only the Whitstable oysters ended their journey on foreign tables.

This is not to give the impression that the roads were empty. The coming of the waggon, in Queen Elizabeth's reign, and the coach, 100 years later, made the amount of traffic borne on the roads intolerable and led eventually to the introduction of a new system—turnpiking—by which a group of local landowners and business men took over a stretch of road from the parish authorities, and undertook by Act of Parliament, to provide a decent highway. Before that, nevertheless, a great deal of passenger and goods traffic was carried along the county's three main roads. Herds of sheep and cattle were driven to Smithfield by drovers from the Weald or Romney Marsh, and the general impression given is one of regular activity and movement. The ruts and mud may have made the stretches, particularly, from Rye to Tonbridge, from Tenterden to Maidstone, and from Hythe to Ashford impassable in many places, but the roads were up to 80 feet across, so you might pick a path round them, and the traveller was even allowed by law to leave the highway altogether and seek a way over private property, if the situation was completely beyond hope.

The London to Hastings road—the 'Rye road'—was the first to be turnpiked, and tolls charged for its upkeep, in 1710. Travellers might travel from London to Rye, along this road, and there take ship for Dieppe. More of the traffic would be of slow, burdened packhorses, carrying wool on the horse's backs, or Sussex fish for Billingsgate. But these were scarcely the reasons for the turnpike, which stopped at Tunbridge Wells, before the worst stretches were reached on the way to the coast. It was rather the fashionable convoys of coaches which left regularly from the West End for the Wells, whose passengers were no longer prepared to tolerate inconvenience or discomfort, which brought about the first real improvement. The London–Dover road was turnpiked for the whole distance to Canterbury by 1750. The stretch from Gravesend to the capital was the last to be completed, which would have pleased the Gravesend long ferry-men, accustomed to meet the Watling Street travellers, including those from Europe, and convey them the last part of their way by water. The other main road to the coast, through Wrotham and Ashford to the dejected Hythe, was not improved till later. The great numbers of Romney Marsh sheep which were driven along it could not have helped its condition.

Hops, Reformation, bays and beer,
Came into England all in a year.

So they told Defoe, and the sight of the hopfields, like that of the fruit orchards, is a theme on which travellers always played. Like many new crops in Kent, hops were introduced from the Low Countries, during the fifteenth century. By 1600 they were becoming quite widespread—around Goudhurst, for instance—and many farmers were planting hop-gardens, along with other crops, on their farms. The gardens were small, of only one or two acres, and the oast houses very different from the round oast with its sloping roof, crowned with a white triangular vent, which we regard as so typical a part of the Kentish scene, but which in fact is a nineteenth-century invention. Before this it was a rectangular building, with a kiln in the middle, and storage space at each end for the dried and undried hops. A great deal of wood had to be available locally for the poles, since the hops were trained to grow round the poles themselves, not, as later, around wires. Here Kent was well supplied, as it was also with men, women, and children to fill the bins during the picking season. Already, in the seventeenth century, paupers were being put to work in the hopfields, though the regular late August invasion of London hoppers did not occur until the last century. By the end of the seventeenth century one-third of England's hops were being produced in Kent. Twenty years later Defoe reported that Canterbury's prosperity depended on hops, and no longer on the textile trade. He had been told, though he found it difficult to believe, that 6,000 acres of hops had been planted about the city within living memory. Yet it was a tricky crop, whose risk was compensated for by the high profits of a good summer.

Kent was famed for its fruit, and by the time of Elizabeth's death, was regarded as England's main fruit producer, particularly of apples, pears, and cherries. Richard Harrys, fruiterer to Henry VIII, had a hand in the start of the county's reputation. According to Lambarde, writing in 1570, Harrys 'did in the year 1533 obtain 105 acres of good ground in the parish of Teynham (between Faversham and Sittingbourne) which he divided into ten parcels and with great care, good choice, and no small labour brought from beyond the seas the sweet cherry, the temperate pippin, and the golden reinette'.

Farmers liked to use the orchards, where the trees would be planted from 20 to 30 feet apart, for pasture. The fruit trees provided shelter for the cattle or the sheep and kept the grass green and damp in hot summers. Celia Fiennes remarked on the cherry orchards near Gravesend, which ran down to the Thames, so that the fruit could go easily to market in London. She refers to 'the Kentish cherries, a good sort of Flemish fruit', a further illustration of the influence of the Low Countries. Defoe described the cherry orchards around Maidstone as the largest in England, and says that the London fruit consignments up the Medway from Maidstone formed a part of a total trade between that town and the capital which exceeded trade from any other market town in England.

Orchards, like hopfields, were small, of two or three acres, and were to be found in particularly large numbers between Gillingham and Faversham. It was here too that the rich wheat fields were to be found, which supplied a large part of London's needs. Like the barley of east Kent and Thanet, it reached London's markets by sea. Cattle were bred and fattened on the Weald, sheep mainly on Romney Marsh where 'lookers' supervised those many herds which belonged to upland farmers. Here many of the county's sheep originated, and about half its wool. It was a desolate area, with a declining population, an introverted people, and a steady flow of wealth draining away to farmers or merchants who lived in sunnier parts of the county. As for its flooded roads, when they were not made impassable by pot holes, they were blocked with sheep being nudged, cajoled and driven to Ashford or Tenterden markets, or perhaps further afield to Maidstone or to Smithfield.

Kent had even further cause to be grateful to immigrants from Holland and Belgium for the introduction of market gardening. As we have seen, at Sandwich they introduced new types of garden produce in the seventeenth century, particularly carrots and cabbages. To these were added peas, onions, flowers, parsnips and asparagus—as always mainly for the London market—and market-gardening spread during the eighteenth century to north Kent and the areas around Gravesend and Greenwich. Dutch influence was also to be found in the use of turnips and other root crops after the Restoration, along with crops such as sainfoin and clover. Such attempts to restore fertility to the soil without letting it lie merely fallow, and to provide winter feeding for animals, are often described as originating in Eastern England during the eighteenth century, on the estates of great landowners like 'Turnip' Townshend. In fact they were to be found 30 or 40 years earlier in Kent.

These years saw the rise and fall of the Weald as an industrial area and in particular of the Wealden cloth and iron industries. We have seen the origin of the Weald's clothing industry, in the later middle ages around Cranbrook. During the reigns of Elizabeth and James I it reached its height, and survived even the collapse of the Antwerp market through war in the 1570s. But from 1630 it declined quickly before the competition of lighter cloth—'the new draperies' from east Kent or East Anglia—and in 1720 Defoe found only ten clothiers in the whole of the county. The ordinary place of production remained the home, though special processes such as fulling, and dyeing were carried out separately, the former often being conducted in mills—as on the Loose river near Maidstone—the latter in the clothier's workhouse. A weaver would probably have two looms in his home, placed in the 'shop', leading off the hall, or in one of the upstairs rooms, if the hall was chambered. Like his employer, he combined the textile industry with small-scale farming, on which he fell back in hard times.

The Weald, noted Camden, the Elizabethan historian, towards

the end of the sixteenth century, was full of 'mills . . . beating with hammers upon the iron (which) fill the neighbourhood round about night and day with continued noise'. Sussex had mined and manufactured iron on a larger scale than Kent, but the stimulus of war urged on Kent's Wealden iron masters, who had the necessary iron ore, wood, and running water to hand, the streams often needing only to be dammed. Place names still reveal the presence of the old forges—Hammer Dyke, Furnace Hill, Cinderhill Wood, in the area between Tonbridge and Horsmonden and Lamberhurst. In the woods the charcoal burners who provided the industry's fuel would stay awake for a week on end, while their fires burnt. Their furnace would be as much as 40 feet in diameter, and on top of it they would build a wooden dome, packed on a central pole nine feet high, covered with turf, straw, and a wattle screen. The industry was never a large one; only a dozen furnaces or so would be working at any one time in the county.

On occasion public events impinged during these centuries on ordinary life—but rarely. In 1588, and again at various times in the 1590s, Spanish invasion of the county was expected. The ancient warning system of beacons, originally great bonfires but now tall poles with iron baskets at the top which could burn pitch was carefully organized. There were 30 hill tops within sight of each other; communication between London and the county's south-east coast was maintained through the Medway gap in the North Downs, the beacon standing at Birling. The county was supposed to muster 14,000 men if an invasion threatened, but when Spanish ships were in the Channel in the summer of 1588, only about 3,500 men took arms during the crucial period of 29 July to 19 August.

We have already seen that the gentry were unsympathetic to Charles i's pretensions in the 1630s, and in particular to his attempts to levy ship money without parliament's consent. They were even more opposed to Archbishop Laud's policies in the Church and were keen to curb the power of the bishops. But by 1641—42 they had taken up a moderate position, and in the Kentish Petition of 1642 had expressed their belief that episcopacy should be reformed and not abolished, and their fear that parliament was exceeding its legitimate power. The county was remote from the main centres of military activity during the first civil war, and took little part in the fighting. If feeling was moderately Royalist, it was not militantly so, and it took the high-handed actions of the Parliamentary County Committee under the unpopular Sir Anthony Weldon, which seemed to challenge the traditional sources of authority, and above all the power of the local gentry, to bring about the troubles in Kent which led to the second civil war in 1648.

The troubles started with a riot at Canterbury, on Christmas day 1647. Parliament had ordered that Christmas should not be observed—it was after all from their point of view a Papist festival whose roots lay in paganism—and the County Committee of Kent issued an order which demanded strict observance of the prohibition throughout the county. The mayor of Canterbury, a brewer, announced a week before Christmas that no church services must be held on 25 December, that there must be no making of 'plum pottage or nativity pies', that the shops must be open and a market held, and that no holly, rosemary, or bay must be hung at street doors. On the day a riot developed. The leaders of the 'rabble' were joined by soldiers and brought two footballs with them into the High Street. They were joined 'on a sudden (by) great numbers of rude persons not only of the city but of country-fellows, strangers from the parts adjacent whereby they speedily grew into a tumult.' They opened up the public houses, perhaps because the Mayor supplied the beer, and 'set up holly-bushes at their doors like your country alehouses, and gave entertainment with, Nothing to pay, and, Welcome gentlemen.' At this point more responsible forces, openly declaring themselves supporters of the King, took over—the cry was raised 'For God, King Charles, and Kent' on the streets—the magazine seized, a thousand men armed, and the city gates shut. The revolt did not last long, and the city soon capitulated. But when the rebels came to be tried in Canterbury, the unpopularity of the Parliamentary cause in Kent soon became obvious again, and a county petition was drawn up, which was deliberately reminiscent of the Petition of 1642. Once again an appeal was made to the county's traditional freedom, by 'the Knights, gentlemen, and franklins of the County of Kent, the most free people of this late flourishing nation', and once again the keynote struck was one of moderation. A treaty was to be made which would settle both the king's and the parliament's just rights; the army was to be disbanded; government was once again

49 *Dover Castle during Cromwell's rule*

to be by law, and 'according to the Petition of Right our property
may not be invaded by any taxes or impositions whatsoever'. The
petition aroused support quickly throughout the county. The
gentry moved into action using all their local influence to arouse
support, and their connections with each other to co-ordinate
action. Men were raised in fairly large numbers over the county,
though chiefly in the centre and east. Everywhere the local
patriotic appeal was used:

> *Retain your pristine prowess and make good*
> *That ancient-line all-uncorrupted blood . . .*
> *That Kentishmen were never conquered yet.*

But the petitioners were their own worst enemies. The social system of the county ensured that there was no one dominant family able to supply a Kentish leader whose authority would be universally accepted, and leadership was meant to be provided by two committees of gentry, one at Canterbury, and one at Rochester, each with 40 or 50 members. They were hopelessly split amongst themselves. Only a minority regarded themselves as Cavaliers; most favoured a moderate settlement, and were prepared to make terms with parliament's commissioners, so long as they were conciliatory. There was widespread feeling against the 'outsiders' who came to join them—Royalists from other parts of the country, some said even from abroad. When Fairfax was sent by Parliament to 'settle the Kentish question' he found the opposition half-hearted, divided, and keen to make peace. Nevertheless his storming of Maidstone was a serious business, in which his 7,000 men were forced to fight for the town street by street, and even house by house. Canterbury and Rochester surrendered easily, and were granted kindly terms. Dover, Deal, Sandown and Walmer Castles had surrendered by August. A landing by the Royalist Duke of York on Thanet with Dutch troops did more harm than good, for it meant that local patriotism was now enlisted on the parliamentary side.

The impact of outside events continued to be felt intermittently. During the Civil War period 88 clergy had been ejected out of a total of about 550 clergy in Kent. After the Restoration 76 refused to accept the new Act of Uniformity. Once again most clergymen had stayed in their parishes during a period of bitter theological conflict. In 1667 the Dutch had revealed the poverty of the county's defences. (In fairness it must be remembered that 20 per cent of

50   *Rochester and Chatham being burned by the Dutch, 1667*

Gravesend's population had died the previous year of the plague, along with 30 per cent of Chatham's.) They sailed up the Thames estuary, destroyed the fort at Sheerness, and made their leisurely way up the Medway. At Chatham they found the town in a state of panic, expecting to be sacked. But the Dutch merely destroyed some ships, and carried off the 'Royal Charles' to Holland, so that Britain's largest warship could be visited by exultant holiday-makers. Twenty-one years later, when James II made his ignominious dash into exile before the armies of Dutch William, he was picked up off Faversham and forced to return to Whitehall. It was said that his captors treated him contemptuously, taking from him £200 in gold, his watch, and his sword, and calling him 'such harsh expressions as old rogue, ugly, lean-jawed, hatchet-faced Jesuit, popish dog etc.'

A hundred years later Napoleon provided a far more serious threat of invasion than any since William the Conqueror's. Small

51 *An 18th century scene by Rowlandson of the Norman Staircase, King's School, Canterbury*

forts, called Martello towers, since they were based on a defence work at Cape Martella in Corsica, were built along the coast from Folkestone, along the Romney Marsh and into Sussex, and many remain today. They housed 25 men, carried a gun on their roof, and held sufficient stores of water, food and ammunition to withstand a siege. Behind them still runs the Royal Military Canal from Hythe to Rye. It was built as a means of moving troops quickly, as well as a line of defence, and behind it again ran a military road. Nine semaphore stations—at night signalling was by lamps—were constructed on the tops of hills, and it was claimed that a message could be sent from Deal to London in two minutes. There was talk of evacuating cattle and other livestock from east Kent, along with the elderly and sick. But the main sign of war to the ordinary citizen lay in the presence of troops, far more in number than ever before. Apart from the barracks at Chatham, Dover, and Shorncliffe, the army camped under canvas on Barham Down, at Brabourne Lees, near Ashford, and at Coxheath to the east of the Medway. It was from this time that the association between Kent and the army began. It is still strong, particularly in the east of the county. Yet such intrusions from outside were rare. Kentish life continued, generation by generation, much the same—a small, short-lived, mainly agricultural population, suspicious of outsiders, and deeply immersed in its own affairs, as it lived out its life in its one-street towns or moved to and fro along its high-hedged lanes.

7
Nineteenth-Century Kent

The Kent that emerged from the wars against Napoleon was still basically agricultural. There were industries, of which the most important was shipbuilding in the royal dockyards at Chatham, where the *Victory* was built, and at Sheerness, but the total number of those industrially employed formed only one-tenth of the agricultural population. The disruption of the early industrial revolution was scarcely experienced in Kent, while the enclosure movement did not effect a county in which the open-field system had never taken root. Yet the county of the post-war years was radically different from that of the eighteenth century. The county which had been thought of traditionally as the home of the prosperous yeoman farmer was being described in 1822 by Lord Brougham as the most depressed county in England.

Kent was brought to a state of open violence by 1830, for the first time since the Civil War, and the most important cause was the rise in population. From 1801 to 1831 Kent's population increased by 56 per cent, and although the increase naturally varied greatly from one part of the county to another, it was true throughout the county that four people were living in the 1830s where three had lived at the beginning of the century. The causes remain obscure—a lower infant mortality rate, perhaps, due to medical advance and an earlier age of marriage—but the effect was dramatic. By 1830 poor law overseers and other parish officers were being bluntly realistic about the future. There was simply not enough work to go round, they said, and young men, particularly if they were unmarried, were encouraged to emigrate. In Lenham—a parish whose situation was investigated by the Royal Commission on the Poor Law in 1833—the authorities had paid the passage of 50 villagers who had agreed to make their way to Quebec, though they reported back from there that work was as hard to find in Canada as it was in Kent. Shortly before, the parish officers of Headcorn must have been toying with similar schemes, for a sea captain who was ready to sail for the same city from Dover wrote to them and offered passages at bargain prices —£4 10s for adults, £2 5s for children. Ten labourers, most of them unmarried, aged between 18 and 30, took up the offer.

Yet the county's problems also had other roots. In common with the rest of the country, farmers had enjoyed high prices for their crops, and particularly for their corn, during the war. Even Romney Marsh had taken to growing corn, a practice which continued after the war, when Cobbett described the Marsh wheat as growing five feet high. But if the farmer had prospered during the war years, the labourers had not. Prices had risen

52 'Want, a View of Rochester in 1856' by Richard Dadd

three times, while farm wages had merely doubled, with the result that the poverty was acute and widespread. In east Kent a labourer, living in a rented cottage, at a rent of £2–£3 a year, would be paid 2s to 2/6 a day for a ten hour day at a time when a quartern loaf might cost as much as 8d, meat 8d–10d a lb., and potatoes 5s for a hundredweight sack. He would rely on the sale of pork or wheat by his farmer at reduced prices, on autumnal or early winter threshing jobs, which would be paid at piece rates, and on work in the hopfields—if he lived in an area where hops were grown—in which all his family would join. But more and more he was forced to rely on poor relief, particularly if he had a number of children.

Other forces were also at work to promote disaffection. The practice by which, as we have seen, many labourers had lived in the farmer's household had largely disappeared during the war, since neither farmer nor labourer liked it. As Cobbett put it: 'Why do not farmers now feed and lodge their workpeople, as they did formerly? Because they cannot keep them upon so little as they give them in wages.'

Mr Hodges, MP, described the changes in the Weald when he spoke to the Select Committee of the House on the Poor Laws in 1831: 'The wages that a servant received in a farmer's family bore

53 *'Boatmen near Chatham' by Thomas Rowlandson*

no proportion to those he got out of it; he became dissatisfied with his situation; and the farmer, in consequence of the alteration of circumstances and the high prices which prevailed during the war, got above his situation and was ready to part with all his men, whom he considered rather incumbrances and annoyances to him; and thus by mutual consent the masters and the labourers parted.'

In the new situation there was little to bind a man to his farmer except money and there was not much of that. The labourer was now hired by the day or by the hour, instead of for three months or even a year. Farm hands, apart from stock hands, became casual labourers, like dock labourers, paid nothing when they were not engaged on a specific job. Their conditions were worst when they relied entirely on the farms for their living, and had no common land or woodland to use as supplements to their wage or parish dole.

Cobbett found that Thanet, which had become a granary for the London market, had become a depressed area, the houses 'beggarly in the extreme' and the people, the women even more than the men, dirty and down-hearted. Here, as elsewhere he found the threshing machines—four at Monkton, three at Sarre —which, since they threatened to take away one of the few remaining winter jobs open to the labourers, were to act as the symbols for their hatred in the 1830 Farm Labourers' Revolt.[1]

1830 was a year in which a number of moods likely to promote disaffection met. There was a general election. In Paris another French Revolution had broken out. In the Weald there had been a drive to reduce poor relief, and rates had been cut. There was heavy unemployment, hop prices fluctuated wildly, and the general mood of desperation, combined with the political radicalism so often attractive to craftsmen, shopkeepers, and yeoman farmers, led to a movement to reduce tithes. Labourer and farmer were at one in their resentment of the parson's tax. Most important of all, was fear of the winter. The harvest of 1829 had been a poor one, and the winter which followed it hard. Now once again the harvest had been poor, and the autumn threatened to be followed by even worse privations. The riots in Marden were said to be caused not only by low wages but by 'fear of the winter'. Round Chislehurst and Sevenoaks it was said that the employment of Irish labourers by local farmers proved the last straw, though no evidence was ever produced that they were in fact at work in the

[1] The account I give of this revolt is based on *Captain Swing* by E. J. Hobsbawm and George Rudé.

View of the JUSTITIA HULK, with the Convicts at Work, near Woolwich.

fields. But it was the use of the threshing machines which finally brought about the revolt. There was little enough work in the winter months in any case, without machines further reducing the labourers' opportunities. When in east Kent, some local farmers decided to use machines against the wishes of many of their number and despite, in the case of Barham, the clear recommendation of the village vestry meeting that the machines should not

145

be used, the trouble became worse than local riot.

From June, arson had been reported in west Kent, and there were sufficient numbers of cases for the authorities to be left in no doubt that the fires were the result of protest incendiarism. By the end of September 20 fires had been reported—chiefly of ricks and barns—around Bromley, Sevenoaks, and Orpington. Gangs from Elham, Lyminge and Stelling Minnis had destroyed machines in Lower Hardres and Upper Hardres near Canterbury, and in the area of Hythe and Folkestone. The gangs which were purposefully roaming the countryside, with blacksmiths and carpenters to the fore as particularly skilled machine-breakers, numbered from 20 to 50 men. They clearly enjoyed the support not only of the desperate but of many farmers and gentry, and when the first seven were brought to court at the East Kent Quarter Sessions the magistrate, Sir Edward Knatchbull, dismissed them with a caution and the minimum sentence of three days in prison. At the same time the fires continued to burn in west Kent, and the *Times* reporter, who covered the county's disturbances fully, reported that the crowds which watched the ricks and farm buildings burn impeded the efforts of the fire brigades or local volunteers to put the fires out. At Orpington the labourers stood by a burning barn and said 'Damn it let it burn, I wish it was the house; we can warm ourselves now; we only want some potatoes; there is a nice fire to cook them by.' Fire hoses and leather pipes were slashed. And on 21 October the first of the famous threatening letters was mentioned by the *Times* reporter. These letters, signed 'Swing', or 'Captain Swing', were often the prelude to an attack ,though the mere receipt of one was generally sufficient to persuade the recipient to take the necessary action—dismiss his Irish labourers, if he had any, or destroy his threshing machines. The arrival of letters like the following with the morning mail was sufficient to terrify all but the most determined:

'Sir,
    This is to acquaint you that if your thrashing machines are not destroyed by you directly we shall commence our labours—signed on behalf of the whole,
                                                                Swing.'

'this is to inform you what you have to undergo Gentlemen if providing you Dont pull down your meshines and rise the poor mens wages the married men give tow and six pence a day, the singel tow shilings or we will burn down your barns and you in them this is the last notis.'

Most of the farms attacked were attacked with a reason. Parsons, as we have seen, tended to be the object of both the labourers' and the farmers' hatred and suffered particularly in the Weald. Their tithe barns, unlike the farmers' ricks and buildings, were often uninsured. Justices who were believed to be particularly harsh on the poor were obvious targets, like Mr Michael Becker, JP, whose property at Ash was fired because of his unfeeling conduct towards the poor. Parson justices were the most hated of all:

'Sir,
Your name is down amongst the Black hearts in the Black Book and this is to advise you and the like of you, who are Parson Justices, to make your wills. Ye have been the Blackguard Enemies of the People on all occasions, Ye have not yet done.

As ye ought
Swing.'

There were reports of military-type organization: flags were carried, horns blown, leaders with white hats rode on white horses, wearing their best clothes. A naval deserter, the allegedly Jacobin Robert Price, led one group. John Adams, the Radical cobbler of Maidstone, led another at East Sutton and Langley; at Ash there was 'Captain' Revell, and in Thanet 'General' Moore of Garlinge. There were wild tales of 'gentlemen' or 'strangers' travelling about in 'Green gigs', firing stacks with incendiary bullets, rockets, or fireballs and distributing sums of money. The county buzzed with rumours of outside agents at work—smugglers, Papists, the agents of Daniel O'Connell, bigoted Protestants, Radicals, foreign revolutionaries, or *agents provocateurs* employed by the government.

The aims of the labourers' bands became now much more positive. The anarchic and vandalistic stage of the revolts was passed, and the men concentrated on an increase of wages to a minimum 2/3d a day in winter and 2/6d a day in summer, with an end to unemployment in the countryside.

In November a gang of men roamed the country around Goudhurst complaining of taxes, rents, tithes, and wealthy men who lived on incomes of £30,000 or £40,000 a year. The magistrates sent for help to Cranbrook, where two troops of cavalry had arrived on 11 November. Sir Robert Peel, the Home Secretary, had been horrified to hear of Sir Edward Knatchbull's clemency, and had despatched troops not only to Cranbrook, but to Canterbury, where the Seventh Dragoon Guards had its headquarters, to Chatham, and to Tunbridge Wells. The Goudhurst men were confronted with 25 dragoons. The Riot Act was read, the leaders taken into custody, and the men dispersed. From this time onwards the movement collapsed quickly and totally. No Special Commissions were established in Kent to try the rebels, as was the case in Hampshire or Wiltshire, but over a 100 rebels were brought to trial in different parts of the county. Twenty-five were acquitted, 48 imprisoned, 52 transported to Australia, and four executed—all for arson. By the mid-1840s all the transported prisoners had been released. Considering the harshness of the contemporary legal machinery it is surprising that the penalties were not more severe.

Some years after the labourers' revolt there occurred in 1838 the Courtenay rising, which provided a sudden strange glimpse into the pinched and introverted world of a Kentish village, close to Canterbury, and astride one of the oldest main roads in England, along which travellers to and from the Continent had travelled for hundreds of years. The last of the Kentish revolts was centred around a Cornishman named John Tom, who called himself Sir William Courtenay, Knight of Malta, and who had been recently released from prison and from a lunatic asylum. Tom had arrived in Canterbury in September 1832, putting up at an inn in the High Street, and calling himself Count Moses Rothschild. With his long black hair and well kept glossy beard, he made a striking sight, as he strolled along the city's streets distributing largesse to children or to the poor, and borrowing even more freely from anyone who could be persuaded to lend. It was the year of the Great Reform Bill, and in December an election—the first to be held on the reformed franchise—was due. Within a few weeks of his arrival Tom had taken on a new *persona*, and declared himself to be 'Sir William Percy Honeywood Courtenay, Knight of Malta, heir to the earldom of Devon, and of the Kentish estates of Sir

Edward Hales, King of the Gypsies, King of Jerusalem.'[2] He was approached to stand as a candidate in the excited, hysterical city, and the *Kentish Observer* described the scene at his nomination as follows: 'At length Sir William, who wore a crimson velvet vest, richly trimmed with gold, and a mantle of the same material, was enabled to make his powerful voice reach to the remotest parts of the Hall. He promised that if they returned him he would reform the House of Commons, and take the burthen of taxation from the shoulders of the poor and industrious classes, and fix it on those of the rich. He further promised a return to the good old days of roast beef and mutton, and plenty of prime, nut brown ale . . .'

At first when the hands were counted, Courtenay was declared one of the two successful candidates, amidst uproarious scenes, and ecstatic applause from his supporters. But his Whig opponents demanded a poll, the declaration of which placed Courtenay a long way bottom, with 375 votes, as against his opponents' totals of 834 and 802. In a fit of euphoria Courtenay declared himself a candidate for the County election—east Kent was now entitled to return two MPs—which took place a fortnight later. Just before Christmas he assembled on the racecourse on Barham Down, along with two Tory and one Whig candidates, who arrived with their labourers and other backers marching to their support in military manner. (The labourers of Sir Edward Knatchbull, Conservative, arrived, 500 strong, with clean smocks, hats marked 'Knatchbull', and cudgels. They were paid 5s a day plus food and unlimited beer.) The banners of each side stood dejected in the rain, but the Whig band struck up *Rule Britannia*. The whole scene, with its retainers, and lords, and fair day atmosphere, was more medieval than befitted the first reformed election. Courtenay was dressed more dramatically than ever, in black velvet tunic with trousers to match, silver epaulettes, a golden cummerbund, bright red stockings, and a crimson, velvet cap. He was as ebullient as always but his appeal to the electorate must by now have worn thin for the returning officer declared his total amount of votes to be three.

Nevertheless, Sir William continued to be something of an attraction wherever he went. He undertook a lecture tour of east Kent, where his presence on the platform drew considerable crowds. But his behaviour grew more and more strange, and in 1833 he faced charges for perjury and swindling. He was im-

[2] P. G. Rogers, *Battle in Bossenden Wood*, which tells the whole Courtenay story in full.

prisoned for a while in the Westgate, Canterbury, while he waited to be brought before the magistrates. When his case was heard in the Guildhall, it was quickly removed to the King's Bench in London, so impossible had grown the uproar from his supporters, who had previously threatened to storm the Westgate. But before the minor charge was brought, he had been sentenced for perjury at Maidstone Assizes to three months in prison and seven years transportation. The prison authorities took stock of him however and, after certification, Courtenay was transferred to the nearby County Lunatic Asylum at Barming Heath. He proved a model patient in the asylum, and was released, towards the end of 1837, to live with his friend George Francis at Fairbrook Farm, Boughton. Here he began to visit local public houses, talk to labourers in the fields or on the roads, and offer peppermints to the local children, riding round the area on a light-grey mare, proving a particularly compelling figure to local women. He became well known in Whitstable and Faversham, but the full force of his mystical appeal was felt only in the parishes of Hernhill and Boughton—under Blean, to the north of the London–Canterbury road, and six miles to the west of Canterbury. When Francis grew frightened by his activities—one day he arrived home with two pistols stuck in his belt—Courtenay left Fairbrook Farm and stayed in the houses of admiring small holders.

At first his talk had been of economic and social grievances—low wages, the differences between rich and poor, the evils of the 1834 Poor Law, whose workings had aroused particular hostility in the neighbourhood. If they would follow him all these ills would be ended. But now, in the winter of 1838, new themes began to enter his strange harangues. Using his great throbbing voice, and his detailed knowledge of the Bible, he would ride into a village on his light-grey mare and announce the word of the Lord:

'And the stars of heaven fell unto the earth, even as a fig tree casteth her untimely figs when she is shaken of a mighty wind.'

At this point he would shoot his pistols into the sky to dislodge the stars. He told a local bailiff's wife, who believed him totally, that Jesus had selected his body for His second coming, that Jesus lived in his heart, and that his body was the temple of the Holy Ghost.

At seven o'clock on the evening of Sunday, 27 May 1838 Sir William held a meeting at Dunkirk, near the top of Boughton

Hill, and 200 people were present. When he had finished his
address he called on his followers to work as usual on the morrow—
he himself would be resting then—but to be ready on Tuesday
morning to forsake all and follow him.

So on Tuesday, 29 May there began the dejected, pointless
little episode which was to cost the lives of more men than the
notorious 'Peterloo' massacre at Manchester, 20 years earlier.
Preceded by a man carrying a pole on which was impaled a loaf
and a standard bearer carrying the Courtenay banner—a rampant
red lion painted on a pale-blue background—30 of his disciples
formed up in Boughton, and sang a hymn.

The Messiah had by now changed into a brown farm labourer's
smock, belted, with the inevitable pistols stuck in the belt, together
with his sword, and a bugle slung from his shoulders. He gave a
blast from his bugle and led his followers into the Second Coming.
All that day, and all of Wednesday too, the little party slouched
about the lanes, but recruited hardly any more supporters.

By the Wednesday evening the local farmers and gentry were
thoroughly alarmed, and a warrant was produced for Courtenay's
arrest. The High Constable of Boughton-under-Blean, a plumber,

set off at 4.30 a.m. on 31 May for Bossenden Farm nearby where Courtenay and his men were known to have spent the night. He was accompanied by his brother, and a petty constable. When they arrived at the farm Courtenay appeared and shot the High Constable's brother at point blank range with one of his pistols. The other two men escaped, and when Courtenay returned to the farm he found his victim still alive. He drove his sword repeatedly into his defenceless body, finished him off with another shot, and screamed at his disciples, watching horrified in the farmyard: 'I am the Saviour of the World! You are my true lambs—every one of you.'

Courtenay and his men must have known that the murder marked the point of no return. When finally a major arrived with three officers and 100 men, Courtenay's band could raise one firearm between them, apart from their leader's pistols. In the fight that followed in Bossenden Wood Sir William and nine of his men were shot dead, together with a lieutenant and a special constable. The major in charge of the operation said that never, in all his professional experience, had he seen such fanatical courage as that shown by this band of 35 men. Soon high prices were being offered for locks of Courtenay's hair, pieces of blood-stained smock, and strips of bark from the tree against which he was supposed to have fallen.

The episode produced national comment. In particular the question was asked: 'How could such ignorance and superstition exist within a few miles of the headquarters of English Christianity, within 50 miles of London, and where the people were surrounded by country gentlemen, of importance and great wealth?'

While these savage experiences were being undergone, a whole new industry had grown up along the Kent coast, that of the seaside holiday. Many developments contributed to its prosperity —among them the belief that seabathing, and the drinking of seawater, conveyed the same recuperative advantages as the taking of the waters at Tunbridge Wells or Bath.

The move to the sea grew with the rise of big cities. When all men, other than Londoners, were countrymen Nature in its wildest manifestations—forests, mountains, stormy seas—was shunned. But the eighteenth century saw a change of attitudes, and by the 1720s seabathing had begun at Margate. Ten years later warm sea-water baths were being offered to the public on the Marine Terrace, Margate, and by 1753 the bathing machine had been perfected. (Previously, tilted carts for bathing were the accepted means of crossing the fine Margate sands to reach the sea). Next year we read of seawater drinking, and a building boom began in the 1760s. In 1769 Cecil Square was finished, and a new Assembly Rooms opened containing card rooms, billiard rooms, coffee rooms, noble facilities for dancing, and two circulating libraries—a seaside spa, tailor-made to suit the tastes of 'the quality'.

Although Margate was later to make its reputation as a working-class resort the little port until the middle of the nineteenth century appealed to the middle and upper classes. The *Gentleman's Magazine* as early as 1770 was singing the praises of this first of English seaside resorts. It referred to the extraordinary purity of the water, so different from other resorts, and explained this by the fortunate situation enjoyed by 'this once insignificant village'.

The water was not only fresh but calm, because of the prevailing winds which blew from the land, whereas in the rest of southern England, from the North Foreland to Land's End, resorts were situated on a lee shore, 'which not only makes the water there foul and thick, but annoys, intimidates, and *spatters* the bathers exceedingly.' But the great attraction is 'the bay wherein the company bathe at Margate which is about half a mile in breadth, and has not its equal in this kingdom, or perhaps any other, for the purpose of bathing. The surface is a fine clean sand, perfectly free from rocks, stones, sea-weed, and all manner of soil and filth; and

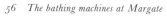
56 The bathing machines at Margate

lies on so gentle and regular a descent, that the sea, at low water, ebbs away about half a mile from the shore.'

The privacy offered by the bathing machine (said to be the best in the Kingdom) was of particular importance. There were machines for men at one end of the beach, and those for women at the other. (The former could be hired, plus 'guide', for a shilling, the latter for 1/3d.) They could best be described as closed horse-drawn caravans, with a door at the rear, and a flight of steps. The bather was driven into the water for about 250 yards, and his entry by means of the steps was concealed from inquisitive eyes by a canvas covering. The machines were, of course, ideally suited to satirical jokes, like the following poem which describes a situation which must have featured in many a bather's fantasy life:

> *But alas! in returning we made a sad blunder*
> *For spying the carriage of old Lady Dunder*
> *We thought 'twas our own and so boldly rolled under*
> *But both swimming badly though I much the worst*
> *I can't say for certain which end came up first*
> *When forth from the surface we gracefully burst.*
> *Her ladyship had just rose out of the sea*
> *While her woman was rubbing as brisk as a bee;*
> *When changing position to ease the poor creature*
> *She gazed upon me and the maid upon Peter;*
> *She gazed for a moment, then feigned a convulsion*
> *And called for the carter to cause an expulsion*
> *'Twas lucky we happened the sea to be half in*
> *But scarce could I swim, or poor Peter, for laughing.*

Before 1815 visitors to Margate arrived by hoy, a sailing packet which normally carried corn, but which could also carry up to 100 passengers to the resort from London, for 2s a head. It must have been quite an ordeal, for the journey was reckoned to take 14 hours normally, and could last as long as three days, while the mouth of the Thames estuary can be notoriously rough. When at last the ship was sighted from the new stone pier, recently extended as an indication of Margate's growing volume of traffic, there was a rush of porters and waiters from the hotels and lodging-houses to the places where the visitors were due to disembark. When finally they landed, probably exhausted, certainly shaken by their long voyage they were pounced upon by platoons of hucksters so that the town seemed to resemble Bombay or Kingston, Jamaica, rather than fashionable Margate. The scene clearly brought discredit on the port, for the directors of the pier announced a fine of £5 to be levied on 'any touter . . . molesting the new visitants'.

The visitor from London, and the great majority came from there, who did not feel able to face the prospect of the sea-voyage could rise early and take the stage coach. He would leave London at five or six in the morning, and reach Canterbury in time for afternoon tea. Here he would change into a local coach for the last 15 miles to the sea. The journey was expensive, costing from 16–19s. After 1815 the visitor would probably have chosen the steamboat, for no less than six separate companies competed for the London–Margate traveller's custom at the height of the steamboat era, and over 60,000 passengers arrived in Margate by

57   The arrival of the Hoy at Margate

steamer in the course of a year. The time was cut to under seven hours, and the saloon fare was down to as low as 6s by the middle of the century. The steamboats, not the railways, pioneered day trips at cheap rates, and had the enterprising notion of a 'Husband's Boat', so that father could join mama, and the children (plus the maid) at the weekend. The coming of the railway in the mid-1840s, though it finally ended the stage-coach service, did not force the steamer services to close. They were cheaper than the railways—1/6d a saloon fare from London to Margate in the 1850s, compared to a rail excursion single of 7s second class, though later in the century the London, Chatham, and Dover Company were offering cheap day returns at 3/6d—but of course they could not compete for speed. (By the 1870s the London–Margate run by rail was being covered in its modern time, two hours.) Many preferred, particularly in the summer, to start their holiday by steamer, with its fairground atmosphere, its crammed bars, and the sight of the flat, gaunt Thames marshlands broadening out on either side of them as they dropped down river. Some, preferring to mix their means of travel, would take the train to Southend, and there would make their way down to the pier to catch the General Steam Navigation Company's boat across the great mouth of the estuary to land at Margate pier.

Of all Kent's coastal resorts Gravesend was the town most effected by the steamboat. The town guide-book was, naturally, euphoric:

'The town has a bustling air, and seems to be in a kind of transition state—half sea port, half watering place. Go where you may, you are sure to find shrimps to sell and lodgings to let. . . . Increase and improvement has been the features of its career.'

The attractions which the writer claims for his port are those designed to appeal to the day tripper, or the family who has saved all year to spend a week at most in mean lodgings. There is the Royal Terrace Pier on which he can stroll with his family, with the gardens which lead onto it. There are outdoor concerts in other gardens, a bazaar, donkey trips—a form of seaside entertainment pioneered by Margate libraries—bathing in baths on the canal or on the river, and excursions to the surrounding countryside. There were 23 registered shrimpsellers, and a public house for every 87 people. It was typical Cockney pleasure; energetic, short-lived, vaguely saucy, out of the world of the riverside East

End pubs, or the later music hall, but it went as it had come, with the steamboat.

The success of the steamer services to and from Gravesend led businessmen and property speculators to invest in Herne Bay. Previously, although some well-to-do families from Canterbury had enjoyed bathing there, where it was said that they would enjoy 'a degree of tranquillity unknown to Margate in the bathing season', the general impression of the coast was one of dejection and ill health. Ireland's *History* merely says of the parish that it is 'in a wild desolate country, abounding in wastes, and few commons, with cottages thinly interspersed. The soil is a stiff clay, mingled in parts with gravel, the water throughout being very brackish.' Houses, streets, hotels, piers, squares, baths were laid out, and it must have seemed that seaside visitors would be bound to repay the investors for their enterprise many times over. But though there was a certain amount of river traffic from London and Gravesend, half of the passengers merely embarked at the

58 Ramsgate Station, July 1864

pier, and took coach to Canterbury, or, increasingly, to Dover. With the coming of the railways to Folkestone, Dover, and the eastern Thanet ports the town stagnated, and streets were left uncompleted, petering out into the marshy countryside in a waste of builders' rubble. Only the railway could save it.

After prolonged agitation the London Chatham and Dover line reached Whitstable and Herne Bay in 1861, and within a generation the population had trebled. By the turn of the century Herne Bay had become a comfortable, middle-class resort, with a regular arrival of day trippers. At Margate this trade had changed the whole nature of the resort, so that the well-to-do had moved elsewhere along the coast, disgusted (said the *Thanet Punch*) by the 'unseemly horse play and obscene language of these hobledehoys', but Herne Bay seems not to have been offended by the presence of London working families enjoying themselves. The town offered good and safe bathing, hot and cold sea baths, good shops and libraries—it is interesting to observe how important a service this was held to be in all seaside towns—an excellent golf course (by now a vital attraction to holiday makers of substance), fast trains to Victoria, good quality hotels along the front, lodging houses everywhere, and of course the famous pier reaching far into the sea, as if hoping to join hands with its rival over the estuary's mouth at Southend.

The middle-class dislike of the tripper was the foundation of the appeal of Westgate and Birchington, which offered a seashore that

59   *Broadstairs early in the 19th century*

approached the quality of Margate's together with a reflective atmosphere in which its beauty could be observed and savoured. The social point was put with typically brutal Victorian force by one enthusiast for Birchington in 1881 : 'The perfect repose of the place is unruffled by the usual noisy seaside attractions. There are no German bands in the gardens, no distressing niggers on the sands, and no revolting donkey drivers in the roads.'

The most spacious and expansive of the county's resorts was—and remains—Folkestone. Broadstairs, of which Dickens was so fond, and where he had a house overlooking the Channel for several years, was select in its company, and possesses a French gaiety and the intimacy of all ports which are snuggled between surrounding cliffs. Dover, keen to become something more than a garrison town and port of embarkation for Europe, had developed as a resort from the eighteenth century, boasting a sheltered shore between Castle hill and Shakespeare's Cliff. In 1817 Marine Parade had been started, and the dignified Waterloo Crescent soon followed. The 'Lord Warden' hotel attracted an aristocratic clientèle known as 'carriage society', which had not previously been drawn to the Kent coast.

The railway made Folkestone. Two years before the line reached the town in 1843, the *Times* was writing: 'A gentleman recently visiting at this place was so much impressed by the dismal, dirty appearance of the houses in some of the narrow streets, that he actually whitewashed the houses on one side of South Street, at his own expense, just by way of example to his neighbours.'

But the South Eastern Railway Company happened, at about this time, to be in serious dispute with the Dover Harbour Board about the situation of their station at Dover and the use of Dover Pier. When Folkestone Harbour was advertised for sale the Company saw its advantages. They would pay no harbour dues if they bought it. They could arrange the train services to suit boat sailings. The price was a mere £18,000. They bought the harbour, which remains today in the hands of British Railways, and were soon offering a service from London to Paris via Folkestone of twelve hours, at a time when other routes to Paris took days. (There was as yet no rail link from Calais to Paris, while the Dover steamboats could take up to fourteen hours to cross the channel, compared to the one and three quarter hours taken by the new railway steamer, running from Folkestone to Boulogne.) Almost immediately the Company built the Pavilion Hotel, the prototype of many later grand hotels, and reckoned to be the best hotel on the South Coast. Folkestone had arrived.

The cross-channel traffic provided a constant spectacle for the excitement and approval not only of visitors to the town but of its own people, who quadrupled their numbers in the years 1841–71. One of the great spectacles was the arrival of the India Mail Boat from Boulogne, bringing with it advance information about Indian market prices for the London Stock Exchange. When its arrival was due all Folkestone would come down to the harbour, dressed in 'Sunday best, tophats and all'.

Dickens loved such Folkestone occasions, and describes one of them in his essay 'Out of Town': 'Now, after infinite bustle, the steamer steams out, and we (on the pier) are all delighted when she rolls as if she would roll her funnel out, and are all disappointed when she don't. Now the other steamer is coming in, and the custom house prepares, and the wharf-labourers assemble, and the hawsers are made ready, and the hotel porters come rattling down with van and truck, eager to begin more olympic games with more luggage.'

60   *An elegant Folkestone hotel in 1910*

61   Market Day at Ashford c. 1850

But it was as a high quality resort that Folkestone, in the years
from 1870 to 1914, became well known. Here the well-to-do and
well connected visitor could enjoy a life of bathing, country walking, promenading, listening to music, gossiping, and eating and
drinking which is sharply reminiscent of Tunbridge Wells in the
days of Beau Nash. The Leas, with its broad walks high up above
the Channel, its bandstands, its great hotels stretching back from
the promenade, like the Hotel Metropole, standing in two and a
half acres of its own grounds, with its ballrooms, banqueting halls,
and billiard rooms, and its rooms for 450 visitors, was the town's
finest creation. From the Leas two lifts—one solely for the guests
of the Metropole Hotel—descended the high cliff to the shore and
the pier. Two bandstands on the Leas proved popular and the
Leas Shelter, where bands could perform under cover in bad
weather, became an even greater attraction.

The Leas Pavilion, catering for the affluent and respectable,
was opened at the turn of the century as a tea room, where a ladies'
string trio provided music. Soon a stage was built, and concert
parties performed twice a day. The whole area was owned (as I

believe it still is) by Lord Radnor, who provided his own police-man, dressed in a blue uniform, with gold-braided peak cap, to patrol the Leas and give it an even weightier tone. As the First World War approached one observer summed up the appeal of Folkestone to Edwardian England: 'Folkestone, since it became a watering place, has always retained a hold on the more moneyed of those who go down to the sea in summer. It does not lay itself out to attract the ephemeral tripper. It even holds itself aloof from the sea, caters for a class that does not sit on the beach, a class that regards the sea with the platonic liking that it confers on person-ages both estimable and *ennuyant*. The air is not impregnated with brine, does not unduly quicken, does not render one embarras-singly boisterous. Hence its attractions for legislators who shun places more marine. . . .'

Here, with the Channel and its shipping spread out below them from the Leas Promenade, as if seen from one of those early flying machines which led by Captain Blériot had recently negotiated the flight from Dover to Calais, the invalid chairs were pushed to and fro, the broughams and later the first Rolls Royces surged up the gravel drives to the great hotels the butler confided the latest scandal about his master to the nanny, and all was well with the world.

Despite these developments at the coast, thousands of Kentish-men continued to earn their living in the traditional ways of agriculture and fishing. Like the rest of the country, Kentish farming was cruelly hit by New World and Australian competition in the second half of the nineteenth century, and saw its early twentieth-century acreage of corn sink to nearly half that of 30 years earlier. For a while hop production rose, particularly in the Maidstone area, but this too suffered from foreign competition. It was thought a particularly insecure method of farming. Sheep-farming was largely unshaken, with the numbers of sheep slightly down to under a million at the turn of the century, and the area of permanent pasture greatly increased. Fruit growing, with the seemingly endless expansion of London's demand and great improvements in transport, prospered as never before. Billingsgate continued to welcome cod, herring and mackerel from Kent's deep-sea fishermen and oysters, shrimps and soles from its waters nearer shore. Yet by 1900 men employed in agriculture had dropped from 47,000 in 1867 to 31,000 and in 150 rural parishes the population had dropped since mid-century. Well before the twentieth century opened, the forces which were so greatly to affect the life of the county in modern times were at work. Industrialisation and suburbanisation had gripped large areas of Kent, and were clearly about to take over many more.

8
Modern Kent

Although Kent was not submerged by the industrial changes of the nineteenth century, in the manner of Lancashire or parts of Staffordshire, and although their effect occurred considerably later its life was radically changed by them. The change can be best expressed in terms of the proportion of town dwellers to countrymen. In 1800 four-fifths of the county lived in the country; in 1850 the proportion between the two was roughly equal; in 1900 four-fifths of the people were townsmen. These changes were brought about either by industrialisation, or by the suburbanisation of north-west Kent, made possible by the growth of fast railway services to London.

Industrialisation has occurred mainly west of the Medway valley, along the Thames, and in the lower valleys of the Cray and the Dart, and in the lower Medway. Here great areas of the county have been transformed by modern industry, and are virtually part of greater London. Indeed when the London County Council was established in 1888 wide areas of metropolitan Kent—Deptford, Greenwich, Woolwich, Lewisham, and Eltham, among others—towns with a long proud past of their own, were transferred to its authority, an official recognition of a fact which had existed for a generation. From Gravesend westwards the whole of Thames-side has become an industrial area broken only by marshes and worked-out chalk pits. It has taken on some of the dejected, abandoned atmosphere of the Thames marshland which it has superseded. In between Gravesend and Dartford the cement industry, which always creates a moon-scape wherever it goes, hacking chalk from the North Downs, scooping the clay from the Thames and Medway estuaries, and covering the landscape with

164

a thick grey powder when it burns the chalk and clay together, became a thriving business.

At Dartford, and later at New Hythe on the Medway where Messrs Reed established their mills in the 1920s, the paper-making industry employed many hundreds of people. The logs and wood-pulp arrived by sea from Canada and the Baltic; London, with its voracious newspaper-reading public, was on the doorstep. In the Dartford–Crayford–Erith area engineering works provided much of the employment, particularly munition-working. Vickers had two great works, and Crayford doubled its population during the First World War as the result of the opening of one of them. Engineering helped too to provide work in the Medway towns and at Maidstone, the dockyards at Chatham and Sheerness employed thousands until the 1950s, while a huge oil refinery was established in the 1920s on the Isle of Grain, which had previously continued in its agricultural way of life, a country oasis between the industrial areas of Thameside and the Medway towns.

Just as much of the county was transformed by suburbanisation. The coming of the railways, and the provision of ample work in London, chiefly of a clerical or administrative kind, changed north-west Kent's life completely. Within a generation at most well-established villages or small country towns had become London dormitory suburbs, their way of life changed as surely as Folkestone's had, by the coming of the railway.

The law of suburban life, that the more important you are the further you live from London and the later you arrive at work, was established early. The Kent suburbs catered particularly for the comfortably-off, and their progress to the station was recalled in his old age by a man who grew up in Penge at the turn of the century: 'Amongst my earliest memories is the hurried but steady procession down to the railway station every morning; the digni-fied bearing, the swift, springy walk, indicating "live wires", the top hats, frock coats, white collars and cuffs. The railway company studied the convenience of these passengers to the extent of cutting a new entrance to the station under the railway track, in order to save 40 seconds of valuable time. A blowsy man with a spongy, unshaven face established himself there and briskly handed them the newspaper of their choice as they hurried by. Arriving at the barrier they would exclaim airily "Season!" leap agilely into the train, and be carried away to the mighty City where they were lost among hundreds of thousands of similar workers who helped to make London the commercial centre of the world. Most of these supers in the great melodrama "Commerce" carried little black gladstone bags, and when I grew older and associated with the irreverent youth of the neighbourhood I was told by one of these young gentlemen that the bags contained "A coupler slices of bread an' dripping for their dinners". This information I record with reserve, however, because the working-class area of the neighbourhood had a great prejudice against the City swells.' (Frederick Willis—*Peace and Dripping Toast*, p. 14)

By 1900 'London Kent' had become the main Kent, and contained one-third of the county's population. In the mid-1960s much of the area was transferred to the Greater London Council, and two new London boroughs were created from it. Bromley, Beckenham, Penge, Orpington and Chislehurst were merged to

62   *Old Beckenham*

form the London Borough of Bromley, and Bexley, Sidcup, Erith, and Crayford became the London Borough of Bexley. Inevitably the life of these old Kentish villages and country towns has become that of suburban dwellers the country over, though they have been keen to preserve what they can of their past against the pressures first of builders and later of road engineers. They have been particularly successful in preserving common and park land for their people, and in preventing the destruction of trees. In this way, in the easy access they offer to unspoilt countryside like the upper Darent valley, and in the large amount of sports clubs to which they offer hospitality, with the break in the rows of suburban streets they provide, these hilly leafy areas of mass housing, with their sudden dramatic views of London, whose streets merge so depressingly with one another, preserve some flavour of their country past. Suddenly, in the midst of uniform streets or shopping centres, one arrives at graceful, dignified eighteenth-century houses or roads, or glimpses, above the plate-glass windows of modern stores, the roof-scape which betrays their Kentish past.

Like every part of England, Kentish life has been that of contrasts. Yeomen farmers of some substance have lived out their lives alongside the families of pauperised labourers, the Folkestone fisherman, dependent on the weather for the difference between destitution and a modest prosperity, has looked up to the Leas and observed the slow satisfied after-luncheon pace of the man who is walking off the effects of a lengthy meal. But there was one juxtaposition which never ceased to arouse both friction and fascination. This was the arrival, at the end of August or the beginning of September, on farms or in village stores and public houses, of the 'hoppers', who stormed, some 60,000 of them at the turn of the century, into the county to pick the hops. For years Kent had established a reputation for hops—in 1906 it produced about two-thirds of the national crop—and a tradition had developed of immigrant pickers. The great majority of them came from London, and arrived for the month's picking with their entire family, including Grandma and Grandpa. Their needs were simple—to earn their keep and their return fare, to enjoy each other's company, to hurl collective defiance at the scandalised villagers who profited so handsomely from their custom, and to enjoy the only holiday of their lives. In return they cheerfully endured the provision of accommodation which would have been

167

63　Happy hoppers towards the end of the 19th century

regarded as inadequate for horses, subsistence wages, which stopped the moment it rained (no uncommon occurrence in September) and an open hostility from Kentishmen which no coloured Londoner would accept peacefully today. (The writer can vividly remember still a sign in one Wealden public house of his acquaintance which was placed in the window one year: 'No dogs or hoppers allowed.') The whole harvest month in the hop areas had about it an atmosphere which sharply distinguished it from that of any other time of the year, and which came out of Hogarth and eighteenth-century London, rather than the century of scientific cultivation. No one who has ever seen it is likely to forget the sight of a Kentish hop-garden at work, the long dappled streets between the bines, the Cockney families filling their bins, with coarse sacking tied round Grandma's enormous waist, the protracted wrangles between checker and picker, the anxious farmer pacing his territory as a captain patrols his bridge. With the mechanisation of picking that has become universal since the 1950s, the sight can no longer be seen. Fortunately the conscience and curiosity of George Orwell drove him to experience hop-picking, and he has left us the story of the 17 days in September 1931 which he spent on Blest's farm at Wateringbury between Maidstone and Tonbridge. Although there are a few twentieth-century touches, Orwell's experience was probably very similar to those of his nineteenth-century or even eighteenth-century predecessors which formed the subject matter for a Victorian popular ballad:

Fine Betsy the bunter from London
From out of St Giles's did prance,
Young Roger the black chimney sweeper
The Grinder and his bonny lass.
They had all been drinking of gin
Till most of their money was spent,
Then agreed to ramble together
To go a hop picking in Kent.

Town Malling it was the first place
The farmer he gave them employ,
They slept all together in a barn,
Like so many hogs in a sty.

Next morning they all met together,
Their tea to get under the hedge,
Their kettle was flung with three sticks
And they all around it did wedge.

When breakfast was over and done,
They all to the hop yard did trip.
Some helped to pull up the poles
And others the hops they did pick.
They spent all the day in great mirth
Not thinking they done any harm,
At night when the day's work was done
Like hogs they run home to the barn.

Orwell's accommodation was much like Betsy's and Roger's:
'... The best quarters on the farm, ironically enough, were disused stables. Most of us slept in round tin huts about ten feet across, with no glass in the windows, and all kinds of holes to let in the wind and rain. The furniture of these huts consisted of a heap of straw and hop-vines, and nothing else. There were four of us in our hut, but in some of them there were seven or eight—rather an advantage really, for it kept the hut warm. Straw is rotten stuff to sleep in (it is much more draughty than hay) and Ginger and I had only a blanket each, so we suffered agonies of cold for the first week; after that we stole enough pokes to keep us warm. The farm gave us free firewood, though not as much as we needed. The water tap was 200 yards away and the latrine the same distance, but it was so filthy that one would have walked a mile sooner than use it. There was a stream where one could do some laundering, but getting a bath in the village would have been about as easy as buying a tame whale.'

The most the pickers earned in practice was 14*s* each a week. This was the wage earned by a family of gypsies, working close to Orwell, who had picked hops every year since they could walk. He himself earned 9*s* a week, enough to cover his keep, his fare back to London on the 'hopper's special', which took nearly five hours to reach London Bridge, and one or two drinks in the Wateringbury public house on a Saturday night, where drinking was conducted in siege conditions. Afterwards the pickers sat round a huge open fire, and roasted apples they had stolen from a nearby orchard.

Twenty years after Orwell's death, his account of his time at Wateringbury was published separately, along with a few most sensible and kindly comments by Mr John Blest the modern owner of the farm in question. Mr Blest points out, a fact which was known also to Orwell, that he had come to the hop-fields in a particularly bad year, when prices were at their lowest, the hops bad, and the weather wet. The pickers were the same as they had always been—chiefly women and children from Bermondsey and Rotherhithe, whose menfolk sometimes came down at weekends. (They were costermongers or general labourers, particularly

64 Cherry pickers still using the traditional ladders

dockers.) They were joined by some local people, and some gypsies.

'Perhaps the greatest character who picked hops on this farm,' writes Mr Blest, 'first came down with her parents when less than a year old, and thereafter never missed a year until she was over 80, latterly making her majestic progress to and from the hop garden in a bath chair propelled by a well-ordered team of grandchildren and great-grandchildren.'

Mr Blest says goodbye to a world that is past in more affectionate tones than Orwell, as befits his superior status in the hop-picking industry: 'Nowadays the clatter of machinery and the revving of tractors have superseded the sounds which Orwell savoured—the laughter and shouts of the children, the howls of the babies, and the bursts of song that could be heard when the sun was shining and the hops were good. For me the greatest change has been in the smells of hop-picking. No more the all embracing effluvium of wood-smoke mingling with the smell of old clothes with their legacies of human odours. Diesel fumes and hot rubber provide a less matey accompaniment to the harvest.'

As the invasion of the hoppers for one month a year produced an automatic response of self-righteous horror from local villagers, so the arrival of the miners, shortly before the First World War, aroused similar reactions. Still, today, though there has been mining in east Kent for 60 years, the sight of the winding towers at Snowdown or Betteshanger collieries rising suddenly out of large unhedged fields of kale or turnips or from great ripened squares of corn seems singularly out of place, while the mining villages appear communities set apart, with their grim blocks of semi-detached houses, and their dominating miners' social clubs. One has every sympathy with the recent correspondent of the *Kentish Gazette* who complained that whenever a local miner was brought to court the case was headlined 'Miner Admits Assault', whereas every other citizen was regarded by the sub-editor as an individual apart from his job, but it is easy to understand how the habit has developed.

For many years nineteenth-century geologists had believed that coal would be found in south-east Kent, but it was not until the government, acting on the advice of the War Office, vetoed further work on the Channel Tunnel in 1882 that borings for coal were begun. The Channel Tunnel works at the foot of

Shakespeare Cliff, Dover, seemed to offer an ideal opportunity for such experiment, and in 1890 coal was found. During the next 20 years some 40 borings were made in the inverted triangle which extends from Dover at its base to Ramsgate in the north-east and Canterbury in the north-west. Miners were imported from the Midlands, the North—especially Yorkshire—and from Wales, who, together with local casual labourers and the inevitable Irish 'navvies' travelled from one boring to the next, and in the end Tilmanstone and Snowdown collieries started production shortly before the outbreak of the First World War. Chislet colliery opened four years later, and Betteshanger in 1927. Today Chislet is closed, and there is talk of abandoning the whole coalfield altogether, since it is consistently uneconomic. The post-war dreams of 'transforming the Garden of England into one vast coalfield'—as the *Dover Express* of July 1921 expressed it—or of opening 18 collieries, with 70,000 additional workers and a consequent doubling of the population in east Kent, which Professor Abercrombie had forecast in a regional survey, have faded away.

The men came almost entirely from outside the county, and brought with them, like their employers, the entrenched attitudes and the atmosphere of industrial warfare of the British coal industry. Kent coal mirrored the bitter hostilities of the national industry between the wars, with skirmishes between pickets, blacklegs, and police at Nonington (Snowdown Colliery) in 1921, one-third of east-Kent miners unemployed during the Tilmanstone and Chislet lock-outs of 1924, and fights between unionised workers and voluntary hands employed by the cross-channel shipping companies during the period of the General Strike in 1926. After the Strike had collapsed, and the owners had locked out the miners, they and their families survived only through private charities, to which local people appear to have subscribed despite their hostility to the presence of miners, relief from public funds, and the onset of the fruit picking and hop picking seasons, for there was little strike pay. When these harvests were completed, the men drifted back to work.

By national standards the wages in the Kent coalfield were good, though the accident rate was high, and the working conditions more than usually arduous. After the return to work at the end of 1926, and the opening of Betteshanger colliery the next year, men came to east Kent from other British coalfields in much greater numbers. Here, at least, work was to be had, and the management of Tilmanstone Colliery actually advertised in Northern and Midland newspapers for 2,000 workers. Men sold their possessions to raise the rail fare, and 200 miners walked from South Wales or St Helen's (Lancashire). The labour force doubled to reach about 5,000 by 1930 but the advertisements had produced a glut of applicants, and many were turned away. Others, horrified by the heat and the humidity of the pits, returned home. Some of those who stayed, according to the secretary of the Kent branch of the National Union of Mineworkers in 1971, who himself came to Kent in 1930 from Staffordshire, were men who had changed their names: 'A lot of the men who came were militants from 1921 and 1926, men who were prepared to stand up and be counted. They were black-booked in the collieries and couldn't get jobs, so they came to Kent with assumed names.'

The conditions at the coal face seem to have shocked men who were accustomed to hardship and great danger in their own coalfields. 'Conditions did improve slightly in the 1930's,' recalls a Welshman. 'But they were still well behind Wales. The heat and the water—you had to lift your shoes to drain them out.' A Yorkshireman who came to Kent in 1929 remembers the work vividly: 'The water seemed to come down faster than the Thames. In the headings it used to flood a yard deep. Where the face had dropped down, you might get four foot of coal at one end, two foot at the other. It wasn't a universal seam as you get in Yorkshire or Wales. The seams rolled about like waves.'

At the face the men wore nothing but a belt and clogs, and some would take as much as eight pints of water with them on the shift. Men living this sort of life are bound to become men apart, particularly if they are housed, as were the married men, in colliers' houses owned by the company. For the owners, by the standards of the day, had been good employers, at least over housing, and had built well-constructed if grim-looking houses in the mining villages of Aylesham, Elvington, and Hersden. Single men faced prejudice in their search for lodgings locally. Prices were raised for a mining applicant, or he might see the addition 'No miners need apply' at the end of an advertisement. Some shops refused to serve this outcast band, and local landowners complained that the worst poachers were always the miners.

The First World War engulfed Kent, as it engulfed the country, with appalling speed. The first week of August saw the usual seaside holiday crowds in the resorts. Within a few days of the declaration of war on 4 August, 1914, they had gone, driven by the homing instinct that accompanies the realisation of most national tragedies, or perhaps, more prosaically, by fear of German naval bombardment. The next to depart were the German waiters and cooks in the hotels and boarding houses. And then into Folkestone there came the first small ships—fishing boats, and coastal colliers —carrying Belgian refugees, fleeing the German army which struck deep into Belgium, occupied Ostend and Zeebrugge, and threatened the north-French coast. They were the first of many, men, women and children of all ages, mainly civilians, but also sodiers separated from their units as they retreated. Before the year was out more than 60,000 refugees had been landed at the harbour—three times the port's normal population—and at one time about 20,000 of them were being accommodated in the town. As the war on the Western Front settled down into a terrible pointless war of attrition Folkestone became a vast transit camp. Thousands of singing soldiers swung down the steep road from the station to the cross-channel ferries daily, loaded with full kit, and due to be carried, in many cases, straight to the front after embarkation in Boulogne.

Another ferry port had a much older past and a more secret modern use—Richborough. Here the area of the old Roman base was used, in conditions of the strictest secrecy, for assembling the enormous consignments of shells and ammunition together with guns and tanks which were loaded into railway wagons from the munitions factories and carried by rail to Richborough. From Sandwich Haven the train ferries crossed the Channel, and their contents were taken to a secret dump on the depressed sand dunes of Camiers near Calais whence they were despatched to the front.

The job of convoying these maritime powder barrels, as of guaranteeing the safety of the men who sailed around the clock from Folkestone, fell to the men of the Dover Patrol, and of the Sixth Destroyer Flotilla based on Dover. From Dover too were launched the attacks on the German U-boat bases at Ostend and Zeebrugge, whose position was potentially so dangerous to the traffic in the Straits, and much of the minelaying which sealed off the Channel from the North Sea. The memorial to the men of the Patrol who lost their lives stands today above Saint Margaret's Bay and can be seen from far out in the Channel. It seems surprising that more attempts were not made by the Germans either to bomb Dover from the air or to bombard it from the sea, but though air raids from both aircraft and Zeppelins took place, in which over 20 people were killed during the war, together with 'tip and run' shelling by destroyers, the damage was never more than superficial. Dover's people took refuge in large caverns, excavated out of chalk under the Western Heights, and running deep into the white cliffs. Here benches were fixed along the walls, ventilation was good, and the sexes separated. Ramsgate and Margate were also shelled, but the worst experience of bombing was endured by Folkestone. In the course of a daylight raid in 1917 one bomb fell at a busy shopping time in Tontine Street, killing 71 and injuring 94.

The first sign of the Second World War in Kent was to be seen several years before it started, in the 1930s, when Richborough Camp was again given a modern use. This time it offered hospitality to Jewish refugees from Germany.

At first the county seemed wearily to be continuing the First World War where it had ended. Troops left Folkestone and Dover in their thousands, while destroyers and motor torpedo boats, a more modern touch, slipped quietly out of Dover harbour at night for convoy duty, or for raids on north German coastal shipping. Then, once again suddenly, the violent impact of modern war was felt. The British army, together with French forces, fell desperately back on Dunkirk in May 1940 and all along the Kent coast volunteers were asked to sail their private ships across the calm Channel to ferry men from the beaches to the transports lying off shore. Others volunteered to work as stretcher bearers on beaches and thousands more helped at the Thanet ports, at Folkestone, or at Dover, where the 338,000 men evacuated during the nine days of the Dunkirk operation crawled ashore, dazed by shock, bewildered by the break-down in organisation, and telling, in some cases, distressing tales of indiscipline and panic. Kent in a few short weeks woke up to the prospect of imminent invasion.

We know now that the German invasion plan envisaged the landing of nine divisions of the first wave, four of which were to be

177

landed between Folkestone and Hastings along the shores of Romney Marsh, two between Bexhill and Eastbourne, and three between Beachy Head and Brighton. Paratroopers were to take the high ground north of Folkestone and block the Canterbury-Folkestone road. The bridgehead was to be expanded inland as soon as possible to a line drawn from Canterbury to Ashford, from Ashford to Tenterden, and from Tenterden to Etchingham in East Sussex.

All along the coast the barbed wire stretched across the beaches and pill boxes covered possible landings. The civilian population was encouraged to evacuate, though never forced to do so. About half Sandwich's population left which may be taken as typical of the immediate invasion area. It was made clear, however, that once a landing started the order to civilians to 'stay put' would be most strictly enforced, to prevent civilian use of roads and railways needed by the army. The roads were closely guarded, and junctions or other strategic points covered by pill boxes or machine gun posts. Houses which the Germans might covet as headquarters were mined, as were important bridges, and elaborate underground hideouts were constructed, particularly in chalky soil, under the direction of the explorer Captain Peter Fleming who was in command of the county's 'auxiliary unit'. This was a group of determined and unorthodox men, soldiers and civilians, who were ordered to form the core of a British Resistance should the county be invaded. Their headquarters was in a farmhouse called the Garth, above Bilting, on the North Downs, north of the Ashford-Canterbury road. Here Captain Fleming packed a barn from end to end with explosives, ammunition, and weapons —the more bizarre the better—concocted schemes worthy of his brother's hero James Bond, trained men secretly on the hills about the Garth, and designed hideouts which even the best German field glass would pass over. To enter one such underground base the visitor had to find a marble hidden in some leaves, insert the marble into a mousehole and wait for it to roll down a 12 foot pipe and fall into a tin can, the signal to the men underground to open the trap door. Another was specially built by a company of Welsh miners where the Folkestone road joins the A2 from Dover to Canterbury while a third was built on the top of Charing Hill where the road junction with the A20 could be watched.

Fortunately, the plans were never tested. The Germans lost the Battle of Britain, and the county settled down to a long bombardment by plane, shell, flying bomb, and rocket, in which 21,000 civilian casualties were recorded, and something under 3,000 civilians killed.

The first daylight raids on Kentish towns occurred in the autumn of 1940, and from then on Canterbury, the Medway towns, Maidstone, Folkestone, Margate, Ramsgate, Dover, Deal, Hythe and other towns were frequently attacked. Much the worst experience in a single night was that suffered by Canterbury on the night of 31 May–1 June, 1942, when 6,000 incendiary bombs were dropped by the German Air Force in a raid which was supposed to have been ordered in revenge for the RAF's recent 1,000 bomber raid on the cathedral city of Cologne. About six acres of the city were gutted—one-fifth of Canterbury—and it seems extraordinary in the circumstances that the cathedral survived unharmed and only 42 people were killed. Shelling was suffered from the French coast by Margate, Ramsgate, Broadstairs, Deal and Folkestone, but Dover was much the worst hit by long range artillery which, unlike bombing aircraft, gave no warning moments to its victims in which they could seek cover. Shortly after D-Day in a night of heavy shelling guns from Cap Gris Nez were landing shells as far inland as Maidstone, 55 miles away.

Kent's ports were not used for the D-Day invasion fleets, though the dummy invasion fleet which was constructed along the south-east coast seems completely to have misled the German High Command, and to have given it to believe that the main weight of the allied attack would fall on the Pas de Calais. From April 1944 a smokescreen was placed over Richborough, where a large part of the Mulberry Harbour, later to be assembled off the D-Day beaches, was being prepared. But the summer of 1944 brought a new danger to the county just when the end of the war seemed at last to be approaching. Shortly after the D-Day landings of early June, jet-propelled pilotless planes, carrying explosive warheads, began to fly over the Channel from bases in north France and Belgium and head for London. Fighter Command, whose planes were comfortably faster than these flying-bombs, had orders to destroy them over the most sparsely populated parts of Kent, and above all before they reached London's southern suburbs. In this they were most successful, often pushing the bombs off course with the wings of their own aircraft, and the rural public grew blasé as they watched the pilots chase the bombs, only to wake up to sudden reality when the chug-chug suddenly stopped, the engine cut out, and spectators dived for cover. Two particularly horrifying hits were scored by the bombs. At Crockham Hill an evacuation centre for London County Council children received a direct hit. Twenty-two children out of 30 — all under five—were killed along with eight out of the 11 staff. At Beckenham a restaurant was hit when it was crowded with customers. Forty-four lives were lost, and the rescue work continued for three days. Seventeen hundred flying bombs in all fell on Kent during that summer when the allied forces were advancing first on Paris and then on the Rhine. In September a new and more frightening attack began, this time by rocket which, like the shells that whined their way across the Channel, gave its enemies no notice of its arrival. Once again Kent took the main weight of the bombardment, and this time, since there was no possible means of diversion, it was the heavily populated north and north-west Kent which suffered most. Both the first and the last rocket fell on Orpington, the latter within a few weeks of the end of the war, Erith was heavily hit, and at Bromley a public house was destroyed where 26 lives were lost. Considering the amount of explosive which fell on Kent during the five-and-a-half years of war, it is remarkable that the loss of life was not far higher.

The county's development since 1945 has followed along many of the lines which were apparent before the war. Industrialisation has spread from outer London to the Medway. Electrification of main lines to London has further extended the range of suburbanisation. London's influence is dominant deep into the Weald, and the morning trains from Ashford or Paddock Wood seem to carry very much the same sorts of people as those from Orpington or Bromley. The holiday resorts may have had to face a dwindling demand from day trippers or from regular seaside visitors, who prefer now to take a chartered flight to Majorca or to the Riviera, but they have housed many thousands of retired couples who have fulfilled a lifetime's ambition by leaving London when their pension matured to spend the rest of their lives at Herne Bay. Everywhere caravan sites are to be found. The watch towers at Reculver, which provided a landmark to so many ships as they

65 *Transport progress!*

rounded the North Foreland to start on the long voyage up the Thames, are surrounded by a particularly hideous caravan village, and much of the coast of Romney Marsh has been walled by them. Developments in fruit farming have altered the appearance of the Kent countryside. The modern farmer will grow fruit trees whose branches can be reached from a stepladder, and the old apple orchard with its gnarled trunks and its arcaded walks roofed by a foam of pink apple blossom is in danger of becoming a

66   Commuters in
heated argument at
London Bridge during a
rail go-slow

memory. There may be fewer day trippers from London to the Kent coast, but far more Continental visitors land each summer's day than ever did before. They arrive in their thousands at Folkestone or Dover to be greeted by posters from Marks and Spencer and other stores, advertising bargain clothes' sales, perhaps to be driven for a quick visit to Canterbury Cathedral squeezed between shopping sessions. Well before Britain had officially joined the European Economic Community the towns of east Kent in high summer were thronged with Continental visitors, while its inadequate roads have been bombarded by great container lorries which have been driven long distances from Eastern as well as Western Europe, and even from Turkey and the Middle East, to deliver their cargoes direct to the customer in the Midlands, London, or the industrial North. A final decision

67   *Village cricket at Leigh near Maidstone*

would now appear at last to have been taken to build a railway tunnel under the Channel, so that an idea, originally propounded 100 years ago, might soon be approaching completion. One can only hope that the fears which envisage the transformation of the country surrounding Cheriton, near Folkestone, the tunnel's proposed terminus, into a vast service station, surrounded by ever-widening areas of suburbia, will prove ill founded.

Yet much of Kent continues to lead a life which derives from its past, lived in small personal units, large villages or country towns. In this the motor car has helped as well as hindered by making it possible for families to avoid big town life despite the employment of their adult members in business or industry. A visit to a weekend cricket match at which the county eleven is involved provides a good example of that fusion between past and present which modern Kentish life provides at its best. In the midst of modern towns the flags fly from the white tents which surround the grounds in the way they have done for a 100 years or more, while spectators sit on the rough wooden benches at Mote Park, Maidstone, in front of the rhododendron bushes in June bloom at Tunbridge Wells, by the famous tree which stands inside the boundary of the Saint Lawrence ground at Canterbury, or on the banks above the Dover ground with the field spread out below them like a Roman arena, in the manner of their grandfathers.

There is little real poverty in Kent and outside the London fringe few large factories are to be found. The sea, and the countryside, which is still largely unspoilt, are close at hand. Though the county will have to fight increasingly hard to preserve its identity, much of its life still shows the independence, the community feeling and the vitality which have characterised its past.

Bibliography

In General

F. W. Jessup, *A History of Kent*
F. W. Jessup, *Kent History Illustrated*
R. F. Jessup, *Kent—County Archaeologies*
The Victoria County History of Kent
For a bibliography on the history of Kent, the reader should
obtain F. W. Jessup's *The History of Kent, A Select Bibliography*
published by the Kent Education Committee. The programme
notes printed by BBC Radio Medway to accompany their
1972–3 series on the history of Kent contain a bibliography
compiled by John Whyman, of the University of Kent at
Canterbury.
Archaeologica Cantiana and *Kent Archaeological Review* are the main
journals which concern themselves with Kent's history. The
former, published by the Kent Archaeological Society, has
appeared annually since the middle of the nineteenth century.

CHAPTER ONE—THE EARLIEST TIMES

Frank Jenkins, *Men of Kent Before the Romans—Cantium in the
    Early Iron Age* (Canterbury Archaeological Society 1962)
J. H. Evans, 'Kentish Megalith Types', *Archaeologica Cantiana*,
    1951
Harrison, 'Prehistoric Oldbury', *Archaeologica Cantiana*, 1933
R. F. Jessup, *'Julliberrie's Grave'*, *Antiquaries' Journal*, 1939

CHAPTER TWO—ROMAN KENT

G. W. Meates, *Lullingstone Roman Villa*
G. W. Meates, *Lullingstone Roman Villa, Kent*, HMSO Guide
W. S. Penn, *The Roman Town at Springhead*, Gravesend Historical
    Society
Brian Philp, *The Roman Fort at Reculver*, Reculver Excavation
    Group
J. P. Bushe-Fox, *Richborough Castle, Kent*, HMSO Guide
Sheppard Frere, *Roman Canterbury*, Town Clerk, Canterbury
Articles on recent excavations conducted at Dover, Darenth,
Eccles and elsewhere are to be found in recent copies of the

Kent Archaeological Review and of County Archaeology (1968 onwards).
G. P. Walker's 'Villages on the Wantsum Channel' (Archaeologica Cantiana, 1932) should be consulted along with other articles on the Wantsum Channel by the same author in A C, Vols XXXVIII–IX.

CHAPTER THREE—ANGLO-SAXON KENT

In General
Bede's, *Ecclesiastical History* Ed. Cosgrave and Mynors, Oxford 1969
The Anglo-Saxon Chronicle Ed. Dorothy Whitelock, Eyre and Spottiswoode, 1969
Margaret Deanesley, *The Pre-Conquest Church in England*
M. and C. H. B. Quennell, *Everyday Life in Roman and Anglo-Saxon Times*
Dorothy Whitelock, *The Beginnings of English Society*
P. G. Blair, *Introduction to Anglo-Saxon England*
John Thrupp, *Anglo-Saxon Home*
Ekwall, Eilert, *The Concise Oxford Dictionary of English Place Names*

In Particular
Wooldridge and Goldring, *The Weald*
J. E. A. Jolliffe, *Pre-Feudal England—The Jutes*
Richard Parker, *The Sword of Ganelon*, Cedric Chivers 1970. A remarkable historical novel about Kent at the time of the Danish invasions.
Robert Furley, 'Outline of the History of Romney Marsh', *Archaeologica Cantiana* 1880 Vol XIII.

CHAPTER FOUR—MEDIEVAL KENT

In General
Ed. Darby and Campbell, *Domesday Geography of South East England* Chapter X
R. J. Adam, *A Conquest of England, The Coming of The Normans*

In Particular
R. A. L. Smith, *Canterbury Cathedral Priory* (For a picture of the life of Christ Church Priory, Canterbury, and of the administration of its estates e.g. on Romney Marsh).

Dorothy Gardiner, *Historic Haven, Story of Sandwich*
R. F. and F. W. Jessup, *The Cinque Ports*
S. P. H. Statham, *The History of the Castle Town, and Port of Dover*, Longmans, 1899
William Urry, *Canterbury under the Angevin Kings*
Charles Cotton, *The Grey Friars of Canterbury*
Richard Winston, *Becket*
C. E. Woodruff, 'Financial Aspect of the Cult of St Thomas of Canterbury', *Archaeologica Cantiana* 1932
C. C. R. Pile, *Cranbrook, a Wealden Town* Cranbrook Local History Society
For Peasants' Revolt: C. Oman's *Political History of England* Vol IV, 1377–1485 Articles in Dictionary of National Biography on John Ball and Wat Tyler
For Cade's Rebellion: D N B article on John Cade
Helen M. Lyle, *Rebellion of Jack Cade* Historical Association Pamphlet
For Wealden Industry: Straker *Wealden Iron*

CHAPTER FIVE—KENT DURING THE REFORMATION

David Knowles, *The Religious Orders in England*
Ridley, *Thomas Cranmer*
Timpson, *Church History of Kent*
D N B articles on Sir Thomas Wyatt and Elizabeth Barton
C. R. Councer, 'Dissolution of Kentish Monasteries' *Archaeologica Cantiana* 1935
C. E. Woodruff, 'Original Documents about the Reformation', *Archaeologica Cantiana* 1915

CHAPTER SIX—KENT FROM SIXTEENTH TO EIGHTEENTH CENTURIES

Alan Everitt, *Community of Kent and the Great Rebellion 1640–60*
C. W. Chalklin, *Seventeenth Century Kent*
Ed. Melling *Kentish Sources III*: 'Aspects of Agriculture and Industry' (Kent C.C.)
Kentish Sources V: 'Some Kentish Houses' (Kent C.C.)
Kentish Sources I: 'Some Roads and Bridges' (Kent C.C.)

Guidebooks to Penshurst Place and Knole House
C. C. R. Pile, *Cranbrook Broadcloth and the Cloth Makers*,
Cranbrook Local History Society
Martyn Hepworth, *The Story of the Pantiles*, Pantiles Association,
Tunbridge Wells
Daniel Defoe, *Tour Through the Whole Island of Great Britain*,
Penguin edition
Ed. Christopher Morris, *Journeys of Celia Fiennes*
S. G. McRae and C. P. Burnham, *The Rural Landscape of Kent*,
Wye College, London University

CHAPTER SEVEN — NINETEENTH-CENTURY KENT

Ed. Melling, *Kentish Sources IV*: 'The Poor', Kent C.C.
William Cobbett, *Rural Rides*, Everyman
E. J. Hobsbawm and George Rudé, *Captain Swing*
P. G. Rogers, *The Battle in Bossenden Wood*
W. H. Ireland, *A New and Complete History of the County of Kent*,
4 volumes, 1828
John Whyman, *Kentish Seaside Resorts Before 1900*, Library of
University of Kent
C. H. Bishop, *Folkestone, The Story of a Town*

CHAPTER EIGHT — MODERN KENT

C. H. Bishop, *Folkestone, The Story of a Town*
J. B. Firth, *Dover and the Great War*
Kent C. C., *Kent—County Administration in War* (1946) the
official account of the county's experiences during the
Second World War
Peter Fleming, *Invasion 1940* and David Lampse, *The Last Ditch*
for the county's preparations against invasion
A. E. Ritchie, *The Kent Coalfield*
George Orwell, *Collected Essays, Journalism and Letters*, Vol I for
Orwell's account of his hop-picking experiences in Kent;
George Orwell in Kent, Bridge Books, Wateringbury, Kent,
1970 this is a reprint of Orwell's hop-picking account, with an
introduction by M. Fitzmoran and a postscript by J. Blest,
Home Farm, Wateringbury, Kent

Index